Joos van Cleve,
Jan Provost, Joachim Patenier

Max J. Friedländer

Early Netherlandish Painting

VOLUME IX

PART II

MCMLXXIII

PRAEGER PUBLISHERS, INC.

NEW YORK · WASHINGTON

Max J. Friedländer

Joos van Cleve, Jan Provost, Joachim Patenier

COMMENTS AND NOTES BY

HENRI PAUWELS

ASSISTED BY

MONIQUE GIERTS

TRANSLATION BY

HEINZ NORDEN

MCMLXXIII

PRAEGER PUBLISHERS, INC.

NEW YORK · WASHINGTON

BOOKS THAT MATTER

Published in the United States of America in 1973
by Praeger Publishers, Inc.
111 Fourth Avenue, New York, N.Y. 10003

The original German edition *Die Altniederländische Malerei* was published between 1924 and 1937 by Paul Cassirer, Berlin (Vol. I-XI) and A. W. Sijthoff, Leyden (Vol. XII-XIV).

Published under the direction of Ernest Goldschmidt

Design Frits Stoepman gvn, Amsterdam

Library of Congress Catalog Card Number: 67-13538

Printed in Belgium and in the Netherlands.

This edition is published under the auspices and with the aid of the Governments of Belgium, Germany and the Netherlands within the framework of their Cultural Agreements.

The publishers wish to express their gratitude to the chairman and members of the Committees for the Application of the Cultural Agreements between Belgium, Germany and the Netherlands for granting most valuable aid for research and editorial work, and to address also their sincere thanks to the members of the Advisory Committee, the Administrative Services of International Culture Affairs, the Centre National de Recherches 'Primitifs Flamands', Brussels, the Rijksbureau voor Kunsthistorische Documentatie, The Hague, the editors, the translator and all those who by their work or advice have contributed to the realization of this new edition of Max J. Friedländer's major work.

Table of Contents

PART II

Jan Provost

Let us adjust our view to the year 1510. Having finished the shutters of the Calcar altarpiece (1, Plates 1-6), Jan Joest is working in Haarlem. Joos van Cleve is about to gain a foothold in Antwerp, where Quentin Massys is just executing his major masterpieces. Jan Gossart has recently returned from Italy. Bernart van Orley is preparing to take part in the art life of Brussels. In Bruges, Gerard David stands at the summit of his career. On all these personalities we have thrown light. Yet the total picture remains incomplete, insofar as we have not yet discussed the forces then beginning to assert themselves in Leyden, Delft and Amsterdam, exerting an increasing influence on the Southwest, notably Antwerp.

Other omissions must be made up for as well. It is Jan Provost who merits the most immediate and urgent attention, for he was already in his prime by 1510, having been born presumably in 1465. He made his appearance in Bruges as early as 1494. We owe all our dates in respect of his work in Bruges to the zealous documentary researches of Weale[1]. On the firm ground of his findings, stylistic criticism was subsequently able to build successfully and recreate the identity of a master of much personal ingenuity[2].

Jan Provost came from Mons, in Hainaut, a town in the South of present-day Belgium, close to the French border. He seems to have begun his working life in Valenciennes, where he married Jeanne de Quaroube, widow of Simon Marmion, before 1491. In 1498 he is said to have acquired citizenship in Valenciennes[3]. After the death of his first wife in 1506, he married Magdalene de Zwaef in Bruges, and still later Katharina Bacureins. From the circumstance that he married Simon Marmion's widow, it has been plausibly argued that he was that master's pupil. Stylistic criticism has not so far been able to confirm this assumption.

Jan Provost came to Bruges from a different culture than Gerard David, from a region that was half-French. Before deciding in favour of Bruges, he had tried to settle in Antwerp. A Jan Provost is entered in the guild register of the Schelde port for 1493 as a 'free master'. But on 10the February 1494 he acquired citizenship in Bruges, and he quickly seems to have gained position and prestige in his new home town. We have testimony concerning honorary offices he held in the guild, and of commissions given him by the municipality. He was a *Vinder* in the guild in 1501, 1507, 1509 and 1514, *Gouverneur* in 1511, and *Doyen* in 1519 and 1525. We know of the three marriages, of a son Adrien, born about 1508, who became a painter, and another son, Thomas, who worked in stained glass. According to Weale, Provost died in January 1529.

In the autumn of 1520, Dürer met him in Antwerp and drew his portrait if *Jan Prost van Prück* is the same person as Jan Provost whom the German accompanied to Bruges in April 1521. Dürer actually lived with him and again drew his likeness[4].

In the Bruges accounts for 1524/25 a payment to *Jan Preuvost* is entered for a *Last Judgment*, installed over the mantel in the great chamber of the town hall.

1. *Le Beffroi*, Vol. 4, pp. 205 ff.

2. G. Hulin, *Jan Provost*, reprinted from *Kunst en Leven*, Ghent, 1902.

3. My source is the catalogue of the loan exhibition at Mons, in 1930, p. 18.

4. *Dürers Schriftlicher Nachlass...* ed. by Dr. K. Lange and Dr. F. Fuhse, Halle a/S., 1893, pp. 129, 155, 156, 157.

The following year, the artist received payment for changes and improvements to this work.

The panel has survived—it is in the Bruges municipal museum (156, Plate 169). We thus have a single starting-point for forming a view of Jan Provost, one basis for stylistic analysis. The master received this commission after the death of Gerard David (1523), when he was already almost 60 years old and had been working in Bruges for more than 30 years. In our endeavour to encompass his lifework, we must dig deep, painfully grope our way backwards from this *Last Judgment*.

The panel looks as though it had been drawn out in width. The curving top cuts into the congregation of the saints, who are seated on clouds close above the ground. At the centre, the upper frame sweeps around a bright disc, within which Christ is enthroned as judge upon a rainbow.

We are reminded of Rogier, of Memling, even of Gerard David who, a generation before Provost painted a *Last Judgment* for the Bruges Stadhuis, which has been lost, but which we can reconstruct[5]. Provost's composition is lacking in hieratic symmetry and loftiness, in the sense of inexorable retribution. Van Orley painted a *Last Judgment* for Antwerp at very nearly the same time, achieving a kind of outward monumentality after the Roman model[6]. Provost neither moves nor impresses the viewer, but rather entertains him with a bright and animated spectacle. He tells his story with ingratiating humanity. He shows a mild and tolerant judge, and beside him intercessors to whom nothing human is alien, even though they make a show of their dignity and rank as saints with their beards and solemn attributes.

5. Cf. Vol. VI, I part, p. 77.

6. Cf. Vol. VIII, No. 87, Plates 84, 85.

Hellfire down below on the right fails to terrify us with its dark and indistinct demons. Overall, the Resurrection has the better of it, a joyous emergence into light. The men and women standing or kneeling on the ground are loosely and obliquely scattered in depth and graduated in scale. The large figures that dominate the foreground belong to the elect. To his spoiled and coddled congregation, the painter is preaching of grace and bliss more dramatically than of guilt and damnation, guiding their eye to the charming angel, heavenly servant to one of the women, whom he helps into a white gown set with jewels. The joys of heaven are temptingly depicted—gems, festive dress, beauty.

The saints to either side of the Saviour are shown in loose symmetry, overlapping one another, turned and inclined this way or that, gregariously interlinked. The nudes in the field below are also turned in many directions, in a careful effort to achieve variety while studiously avoiding showing them head-on. In the spatial sense, the master's hand is nimble, inventive and highly skilled.

Movement is vivid, but by fits and starts rather than with a flowing quality. One notes motives that are angular, uncontrolled, laboured. Special attention is devoted to the expressive potential of the hand, shown with stiff fingers, often crossed, closed, affectedly bent, or spread wide.

Drapery swings out like bunting, with approximately parallel folds, or is spread like a sail, the folds radiating as narrow starlike ridges, or framing limbs and bodies in angular patterns, nearly always close-hauled in carefully considered motives and pleasing arrangements.

The figures are stocky, in part perhaps because the panel's limited height constrained the master. The heads seem large. The youthful female faces with their low foreheads, wide cheeks, large mouths and protruding lower lips express a refined, ladylike spirit.

The harmonious palette is fair in its tints, with a silvery sheen, quite different from the warm and heavy colour scale that was then coming in among the followers of David in Bruges.

Since three different versions of the *Last Judgment* by the same hand as the Bruges panel have been found, we are able to bolster our view by comparing the different ways in which Provost met the challenge on each occasion. We can gauge the power of his imagination from the abundance of his pictorial ideas, while those qualities that recur will serve to complete the picture of his personality.

A panel sold at the Nieuwenhuys auction in 1883, ascribed there to *Aeken* and now in the Detroit museum (157, Plate 171), offers a more spacious composition than the Bruges painting. It is squared off at the top, the heavenly tier further separated from the earthly and the group of saints constructed in greater depth. The dense train of the redeemed is escorted by angels towards the left, where St. Peter stands at the edge in the rôle of gatekeeper. On the right is the maw of hell, again following the model of Jerome Bosch. The light falls mainly on the helpful ministrations of the angels. While the whole concept, the types and the formal idiom have undergone little change, not a single pose from the Bruges panel recurs here.

An almost square panel that has reached the Hamburg museum (158, Plate 172) from the Weber collection seems almost like an excerpt from the Bruges composition, simplified and concentrated in form. There are few figures, in close propinquity. The Saviour, passing judgment, is directly above an angel who solicitously escorts to the left one man who is striding ahead. There is an unusual motive —books, papers and scrolls with which the resurrected put forward their claim for mercy. The form is somewhat soft and stringy, perhaps mainly on account of old restoration work.

Despite many differences in arrangement, these three panels form a firmly linked group, done at about the same time, around 1525. A *Last Judgment* exhibited by Vicomte Ruffo de Bonneval at Bruges in 1902 (159, Plate 172) represents a considerable departure and can be accepted only as a work done considerably earlier. Indeed, in view of its frugal composition—each figure standing quite alone—its stiff symmetry, its awkward postures, its lack of grace and sensual charm, its overall aspect of aridity, we are compelled to consider carefully whether we can maintain Provost's authorship. Several significant features, however, tip the scale in his favour, especially male heads with low foreheads, dark eyebrows placed low, and swelling lips, and the very long, bent trumps in the hands of the angels. Once the authorship is acknowledged, the panel gains in importance, for it shows us the master's art at another stage, an earlier phase than in the Bruges *Last Judgment* (156, Plate 169). But before following this trail, which reaches deep into the past, let us consider some of this master's other works, outstanding in size and merit, in which his style appears at full maturity.

A *Madonna in the Clouds* in the Hermitage at Leningrad (177, Plates 182, 183) is pleasing in its grace. Hulin has identified it, probably correctly, as a work that Provost, by documentary evidence, did in 1524, for the altar dedicated to the

prophet Daniel in the church of St. Donatian. The composition achieves the kind of symmetrical order appropriate to its dignified theme, which requires a courtly order of rank for the Queen of Heaven, the prophets and sibyls, and David and Augustus. The pre-Christian men and women turn to the sublime Virgin, close and present in the flesh, to whom their attention is being drawn, and pay her obeisance.
88 She stands freely and easily in space, while the Holy Trinity, four angels, the standing sibyls and the male and female confessors, kneeling or appearing below at half-length, surround her in a lofty, wreathlike oval. The Netherlander eschews the straightforward, spiritualized monumentality of the *Sistine Madonna*, appealing instead to a more naïve and earthy audience, before whom he makes a show of the superhuman, of venerable patriarchal beards, of rich and exotic dress and jewellery. This is a luxurious heaven, full of light and colour.

Provost's individual peculiarities emerge so clearly that anyone familiar with the Bruges *Last Judgment* (156, Plate 169) will scarcely require proof of his authorship. Much is as in that picture—the gentle women, their heads coquettishly inclined, with their smiling, sensual lips, their wide cheeks; the hands with their animated fingers bent at all angles; the creative freedom; the wealth of form.

Two panels from a St. Catherine altarpiece—one in the Antwerp (135, Plate 157), the other in the Rotterdam museum (135, Plate 156)—may serve as further examples. Legends always give scope and occasion to a painter's storytelling propensities, elicit his personality. In the first panel, the one in Rotterdam, the princess stands before her father's throne, debating in a circle of scholars. The group is alarmingly crowded. The heads, sharply graduated in scale, overlap one another in part, are shown in profile and full face in regular alternation. Most strongly emphasized is the plump court dwarf, to the fore at the left, quite irrelevant to the story, but conveying the atmosphere of a court.

The pagan spirit against which St. Catherine struggles is depicted as ostentatious and autocratic, of limited intellectual stature. The saint is enveloped by dull stupidity, stubbornly intractable to enlightenment, reacting to her arguments with open-mouthed indignation, fanaticism, and vehement gestures. Entrenched cynicism in support of the vested power is contrasted with the calm grace of the valiant champion of the faith—whose, figure, by the way, is curiously stocky.

Provost's somewhat voluble epic approach to adventure was not rooted in Bruges tradition but came rather from the South. He demonstrably visited Antwerp in 1521, presumably went there before and on a number of occasions, and to him Quentin Massys was an example to which he looked up. He was familiar with the altarpiece with the *Lamentation* in Antwerp cathedral, and was particularly fascinated by their shutters with their glittering splendour, provocative effects, and sharply delineated characters. This St. Catherine panel of his is reminiscent of Quentin's *Feast of Herod*. Both panels feature the powerful and opulent figure of the bearded, Oriental tyrant[7], the place of Quentin's nimble page being taken by the massive dwarf. Provost's graceful young woman and the dense throng of hysterically agitated men are, in the main, grouped in much the same way as in Quentin's painting and even the caricature heads are imitated.

7. Provost may have gone to the same source as Massys and known Dürer's woodcut from the Apocalypse (B. 61).

We do note an important difference when we compare these two pictures. The Bruges master takes a far more casual approach. He was not nearly so serious and consistent. His grasp of character was less profound, and he was less conscientious towards the visible world.

The secound panel is dominated by the executioner beheading the saint, a massive and muscular figure, combining the brute power of a giant with the mis-shapen lineaments of a dwarf. Behind him and the saint is a press of soldiers. The panel appears to have been trimmed at the bottom and both sides, but seems to have been slightly diminished only in the vertical dimension, if at all.

Here as on many other occasions, the master let his frame ruthlessly crop his groups, achieving the effect of a chance assemblage, enhancing the prominence of the forward figures, and bringing the execution closer to titillate the curious and give them front-row seats, so to speak. The spirit of menacing tyranny is eloquently expressed by the enormous sword in the hands of the executioner, and the over long sceptre held by the mounted commander.

Now that Provost's authenticated *Last Judgment* (156, Plate 169) and a number of works apparently done at the same time—i.e. in his maturity—have allowed his character during this last phase to emerge clearly, I shall try to retrace the road he followed. Beginning at the beginning, I shall first show pictures that seem to fit only equivocally into the context. Only gradually will we find the transition and connection to the known final period. I am afraid I shall have to ask the reader in advance to grant me a measure of trust that the chain I have forged is reasonably firm.

A small panel with a *Crucifixion* (148, Plate 167), which has landed with Herr O. Bondy in Vienna by a devious route from the Felix collection in Leipzig, may be among the master's earliest works[8]. Done between 1490 and 1500—a date supported by the horseman's dress—it would have been painted some 30 years before the *Last Judgment*. We cannot look for striking agreement or close stylistic similarity.

8. Provost was first proposed as the painter of this panel by O. Pächt, when it was exhibited in Vienna in 1930.

At first glance, considering the work as Provost's, we are repelled by its heavy and sluggish style, sparse composition and uncertain postures. But on closer examination, and taking its early origin into account, we find that it is distinguished by certain unconventional aspects. Christ, dark of head, does not hang on the cross in full-face, but is turned a little. One of his feet covers the other. St. John is firmly joined with the Virgin in a pyramid shape. Mary Magdalene embraces the foot of the cross. A mourning woman, shrouded, turns away into the distance. The figures are stumpy, in sacklike clothes. The figures in the background in particular are curiously low—the horseman coming into view above a ridge line, and the figures in an Annunciation that makes up a subsidiary scene in a chamber on the right. A city forms the termination at the back, with cunningly constructed though casually drawn buildings, including tall round and hexagonal towers.

The figures are massive in effect, with contours that do not reach out far. Yet even these thickened forms reveal a striving for refinement, especially the body of Christ on the cross. The figures of the stubby hands are not separated. On the wide expanses of heavy fabric, folds run like raised footpaths, parallel to each other or colliding sharply.

In the collection of Baron Tucher, formerly in Rome, later in Vienna, were three small panels that obviously belong together, a *Scourging of Christ*, a *Crucifixion*, and a *Lamentation* (138, Plates 162, 163). They presented something of a puzzle, not only because of a long and vain search for a likely author[9], but because their fluctuations in style are confusing. The figures differ from one another, especially in their proportions. St. John and the Virgin, under the cross, are very short, the crucified Christ long and narrow. There is an irritating uncertainty in the postures as well. The dancelike stance of the executioners and the fluttering of the kerchiefs in the *Scourging of Christ* are perplexing. Vehement action is expressed by purely outward means, in the style of the Antwerp Mannerists. About 1505, Provost seems to have been fleetingly touched by the prevailing fad.

The crucified Christ resembles the one in the Bondy panel. The slender body hangs from the frontally placed wooden beam in a picturesque pose, turned a little to one side, with the legs partly overlapping and one foot crossing and covering the other. In the background of both the *Crucifixion* and the *Lamentation* rise steep turrets of varied shape, giving us a picture of the master's architectural imagination and contributing not a little towards confirming his authorship. For the most part, Provost's buildings look as though they were cast in metal—they are very narrow and equipped with flying buttresses and pointed finials. They seem to be no more than sights, enclosing no habitable spaces. The critical elements in the faces are the deeply embedded large mouths and dark eyes. The shadow trails over the lids merge with the brows. The eyes are shaped, with 'painterly' softness,' as mere slits, sources for tears. The most dependable hallmark is a veiled expression of sensual charm that hovers over all the changing aspects.

The hands have gained a little in mobility. Now and then the fingers show a hint of those bent, angular configurations that more and more became a mannered accent in Provost's speech.

A Madonna at half-length, in which Hulin has recognized Provost's hand, promises insight into the master's beginnings, but does not keep its promise. A painted *cartellino* in the lower left-hand corner of this panel in the Strasbourg museum (170, Plate 180) carries this inscription: PITTO IN FIANDRA—PRESENTATO AL PERI—AVGNO M RLE NELLANO—1488. Accepting the wording of this dedication, we would have a surprisingly early *terminus ante quem* for the origin of this picture, which is a copy after Rogier[10]. But as a work by Provost—and doubts of his authorship are scarcely admissible—this Madonna cannot have been done before 1488, indeed, any date earlier than 1500 is unlikely, for his formal idiom appears in it in mature form. The complex pattern of the window, with its bull's-eye panes above, its diagonal mullions, its circular centre, its close screen below, the flowerpot on the sill and the needle-sharp spire beyond—all these embellishments are in the master's personal taste. His familiar feminine ideal, moreover, speaks to us from the Virgin's face with convincing clarity. There are several more Madonnas that go back to older models, in a fashion similar to the one in Strasbourg (170, Plate 180), one at half-length in the Edinburgh museum (169, Plate 180), freely done after Rogier, one at full-length in the H. H. Lehman collection at New York (164, Plate 177), indirectly after Rogier[11], and lastly a detail after Jan van Eyck's van der Paele Madonna (173). I regard all these panels as Provost's work, yet in none of them is his personal character so strongly marked, despite the confinement of the hieratic scheme, as in the panel at Strasbourg.

Standing on its own is a Madonna of archaic feeling, which has gone from the

9. Dülberg, in *Frühholländer* (Pls. XXVIII-XXX) describes them as 'works from Leyden (?), about 1505.'

10. For the composition, cf. Vol. II, No. 107, Plate 120.

11. Cf. Vol. IV, No. 84d, Plate 79.

Gotisches Haus in Wörlitz to the Arthur Lehman collection in New York (165, Plate 177). The Virgin, seen rigidly head-on, is seated on a bench of lawn before a dense flower hedge, holding the spindly, angular child on her lap with both hands. Her large head is a pure oval, her face vague in expression and emptily serene. It is held in the same careful symmetry as the tentlike pyramid of her cloak, stiffened by the scaffolding of its folds. Provost was trying to conform to the tradition of Bruges, where lesser masters, like the Master of the Legend of St. Lucy, used a similar approach. Provost, however, was overdoing an ecclesiastical attitude that was at bottom foreign to his nature. His personal signature is seen especially in the Virgin's mouth, and in the hand that grasps the child's foot like a pair of pincers.

There are three *Lamentations* that form a group, one formerly in the Traumann collection at Madrid (149), another formerly in the Schevitsch collection at Paris (150, Plate 167), the third in the Boveri collection at Zurich (151, Plate 167), from the Nemes estate. The figure scale in these pictures is somewhat larger than in the Tucher panels, allowing the types to emerge more clearly.

The upper lips are a wide, straight line, the eyes are dark and opened in a narrow slit, the brows placed low. The pinched and tearful expressions, together with a certain harshness and stiffness in composition, argue in favour of an early date of origin. When we compare a *Lamentation* from the von Back collection, now on the London art market (152, Plate 168), with the panel from the von Nemes collection (151, Plate 167), the growth becomes apparent. The harsh linear contours have given way. The grouping has gained in natural, flowing ease.

The carefully worked panel in London, which is, by the way, in an unusually good state of preservation, deserves the most careful attention. Occupying a middle position in time, it ties together the whole œuvre and confirms that the conclusions of stylistic criticism are correct.

The body of Christ is held by a kneeling, dark-bearded man in such a manner that it appears in frontal view, disposed at a wide, sweeping, gentle angle, forming the focal point of the composition. It arouses compassion, but does not terrify. There is a persistent note of mild and reverberating grief that sounds from all the figures and faces framing the Saviour as in a wreath—the youthful St. John, the Virgin, Mary Magdalene. The bare body is kept within closely held but subtly animated contours. The rigid fingers are bent and contracted in a spasm. One foot, seen from above, is extended straight. The women's faces are modelled in gentle transitions from light to dark, their mouths large, a spent look to their small eyes. Both in composition and expression, the master has reached his goal, found his own personal note. Looking backwards, we begin to understand the aspirations and ambitions presaged in earlier works.

Painted at the same time as this *Lamentation*—about 1510, in my view—is a *Nativity* that has reached the Amsterdam art market (143, Plate 166). In its grouping as well as in the posture and facial type of Joseph it may be loosely associated with Gerard David's Budapest panel[12]. We can scarcely wonder that Provost, in Bruges, was occasionally touched by the master who was dominant there.

12. Cf. Vol. VI, part II, No. 177, Plate 190.

Entering into rivalry with Gerard David, Provost must have sensed the elder master's superiority in terms of sublime tranquillity and harmonious balance, as well as of that powerful mood creator, chiaroscuro. In Bruges, David's work provided the yardstick by which Provost too was measured. The younger man may have felt more independent in spirit, more progressive, freer in his relation to the church—virtues with which he may have hoped to outstrip David; but for the nonce it was a matter of learning the soft cushioning of form, the subtlety of brushwork, that was demanded in Bruges.

92 The *Adoration of the Magi*, in the Deutsches Museum at Berlin (144, Plate 166), is an excellent work by Provost, unfortunately in only an imperfect state of preservation. It is confusingly crowded, however, mainly in consequence of marked variations in figure scale. Tall, long-headed figures emphasize the vertical dimension, as do the over long tree trunks with their sparse foliage. The donor family is jammed between Joseph and the senior king. The large, ladylike face of the Virgin gleams gently like the full moon.

She holds the tiny child in her lap, and from a ring on her finger dangles a gold chain with a piece of jewellery—indeed, other choice ornaments distinguish the regal train with its crowned visitors. The slender figures are unsteady on their feet, yet their movements have a certain angular grace.

The Madonna with which the master is represented in the Rijksmuseum at Amsterdam (178, Plate 184) shares almost all its qualities with this *Adoration*. It shows the Virgin in company of two saints and a donor. Here too the proportions are noteworthy for their height. The men are dark of brow and deep of gaze, their ascetic air softened only by the painter's sense of grace. The donor, a Carthusian abbot, is being commended to the enthroned Virgin by St. John. In the centre is St. Jerome. In the right background is a fenced domestic garden with oblong beds.

This liking for cultivated land, this preference for order adapted to man's needs bespeaks a nature capable of enjoying tangible pleasures down here below. Everywhere, the paths are trodden, man has triumphed over nature run riot. Provost is fond of terminating his spaces in the middelground, by means of a wall, an arbour, a hedge or a trellis. He loves flowerbeds and flowerpots.

Provost the portrait painter can be discerned in his devotional panels, which are not lacking in donor portraits—a good example is the large family on a shuttered altarpiece at Lisbon (123, Plates 142, 143). We have far less success, when we look for independent portraits, distinct from any devotional context. Evidently cut out of an altar shutter is a male portrait in the Johnson collection at Philadelphia (182, Plate 186), to which belongs, as pendant a female portrait that has gone from Genoa to the Rohoncz collection (181, Plate 186). But then, scarcely an individual portrait by David is known either. After Memling's death, the portrait on its own seems to have been little cultivated in Bruges. We must remember that most of Memling's portraits are halves of diptychs and thus spiritually related to the devotional pictures—although they seek to escape from these religious roots in form and composition and set up shop within their own frames. I know of but one such diptych by Provost, with a portrait on one side—the one in the museum of the Bruges Municipal Hospital, showing a *Christ Carrying the Cross* (126, Plate 147), opposite a monk on the right-hand panel who turns towards the Saviour, hands folded in prayer. On the original frame, the date of 1522 is inscribed.

The left panel takes the beholder unawares with a vision inspired by Jerome Bosch. Christ is shown at bust-length in the crowded oblong, turned to the left but facing back to the right, cross on shoulder, hands pressed together with thumbs folded, just above the lower edge. What is left of the background is crowded with four faces, partly covered or cut off by the constricting frame—two mourning women and two diabolically distorted visages. The extreme propinquity exemplifies anxiety as in a nightmare, distilling the quintessence of the Passion.

The donor's head breathes sorrowful devotion. Dark hair droops in strands over his forehead and covers his temples. His darkling brows merge with the shadows weighing down the upper lids within the hollows of the eyes. The mouth is powerful, its corners drawn downwards, a deep indentation over the chin.

Our knowledge of this expressive donor's head gives us the right to add to the œuvre an individual portrait in the Louvre (180, Plate 185), occasionally regarded as a youthful work by Gossart. It represents a clean-shaven, broad-nosed man at bust-length, and can be considered a considerable enrichment of Provost's œuvre. Judging from the hat style, it must have been done about 1520. The massive head, modelled with heavy, rugged shadows along cheeks and chin, somewhat resembles the monk in Bruges. The unusual configuration of the mouth with its bent-down corners invest the wide countenance with an air of vigorous tension. The eyes too are highly characteristic, with their upward-looking pupils and light-coloured, arched and slightly swollen lids, and so are the hands with their crossed thumbs.

There are masters who rise in our esteem, the more we penetrate into their creations. Provost is not among them, and yet he does gain stature as we get to know him. His œuvre is rich in surprises. He prides himself on his originality in pictorial notions. We never encounter copies, replicas, variants. His workshop seems to have been less adapted to assembly-line production than was customary at the time.

He is clever. This may seem like dubious praise for a painter, since it puts him in an intellectual and even literary context. What is meant here is that Provost's imagination begot significant pictorial ideas aplenty. As an example, the Nativity traditionally assembled the Virgin, Joseph and angels on their knees about the child, who lay on the ground on a corner of the Virgin's cloak. It took considerable confidence, not to say audacity, to loosen these hieratic bonds. Provost, however, did modify the motive—in the shutter of an altarpiece in private hands in England (124, Plate 144): Three angels lift the cloak on which the child lies, like a tossing-blanket, and bring him closer to the Virgin. In their hands, the angels carry the instruments of the Passion, to which reference is made in this way.

In another *Nativity*, a tall panel in the possession of Viscount Bearsted in London (142, Plate 164), an ox intrudes obliquely into the picture at the extreme front with head, chest and forelegs, forming a sombre and powerful *repoussoir*. Beside the beast, the infant Jesus is tiny, almost consumed by the light. What is secondary in content has become pictorially the primary element. We are startled by a familiar shape appearing, only in part, at a place where we do not expect it, where we see it at an unusual angle. Provost was given to varying traditional compositions with such bold shifts of accent, such audacious cuts, such picturesque regroupings. Endowed with a richer pictorial imagination than his contemporaries, Provost did less copying than they, at least in his maturity.

Yet a refined taste held in leash the master's proclivity for extremes of form—his figures are either stocky or slender, almost never of ordinary stature—as it did his preference for the secular aspects of his themes. He never makes a show of his knowledge of form, always keeping his eye on the total picture, whether the mood be epic or narrative, or whether it be lyrically musical.

With Provost an enlivening influx from the South entered the stagnant waters of Bruges art. Worldly charm invaded the stillness of the church. If there ever was a Netherlandish Renaissance proper—before the deliberate imitation of Italy—then Jan Provost was, next to Quentin Massys, its major exponent.

Three Bruges Masters with Makeshift Names

I feel under an obligation to round out our picture of the Bruges school, insofar as the surviving pictures allow. I must therefore discuss three further painters, namely:

The so-called Bruges Master of 1500;
The Master of the André Madonna;
The Master of St. Sang.

We know the first one from a large altarpiece in the church of St. Sauveur, showing a *Christ Carrying the Cross*, a *Crucifixion*, and a *Lamentation* (184, Plate 187). The three scenes are not distributed over the panels of a triptych, but are represented on a single panel, side by side in the context of a single landscape—a type of composition quite unfamiliar in the Netherlands but known to us from Westphalian altarpieces. The *Crucifixion*, in essence, is borrowed from an older model, to wit the triptych by the so-called Master of Flémalle, a copy of which is preserved in the Liverpool museum. The original was probably located in Bruges[1]. The Liverpool copy bears the arms of the city of Bruges.

The so-called Master of 1500 took his vehemently contorted Thieves from the shutter of that triptych, as he did the soldier standing by the cross of the Bad Thief, and the group consisting of the Virgin and St. John from the centre panel. In an access of borrowing, moreover, he also plundered Memling and Dürer[2]. The mounted leader is from the *Crucifixion* in Dürer's Large Passion. That woodcut was done before 1500, although the Passion was not published until 1511. Thus it is unlikely the Netherlander could have had the sheet in his hands prior to 1511. This calls into doubt the date after which the master has been named; it is supposed to have been on the frame.

Detailed in a dry and indolent spirit, the Passion takes on an air of sulky melancholy. The bare daylight and the cool and opaque tints are in accord with the formal idiom. The landscape is in the spirit of the age—assuming now that the painting was done about 1515. It is simple in character, whith a deep horizon full of wide horizontal features. The manner in which it is appended to the cunningly improvised figure composition reveals independent powers of observation. The female types are reminiscent of Quentin Massys rather than Gerard David.

Oddly enough, no other works by this master have been identified, except a panel in the National Gallery at London, a *Christ Presented to the People* (185, Plate 188), borrowed in part from an engraving by Schongauer (B. 15); and a *Miracle of St. Anthony* in the Prado, two works I ascribed to him as long age as 1902.

The *Miracle of St. Anthony* in Madrid (186, Plate 188) is of very clean workmanship. The master here puts his best foot forward. The rather bare pedantry that is his distinguishing mark is particularly notable. The scene is a market square, shown at a high line of sight, its bright, steep cobblestone paving elaborated with painstaking regularity. The youthful St. Anthony kneels before the hamper in which is bedded the gleaming host, worshipped by the ass. Behind the saint is a monk, of

1. Cf. Vol. IV, pp. 12, 13.

2. Cf. J. Held, *Dürers Wirkung auf die Niederländische Kunst seiner Zeit*, The Hague, 1931, p. 77.

portrait aspect, the finest head in the picture, perhaps the donor. At left stand three men, one of whom has doffed his hat and is gazing down with evident emotion at the miracle the other two are excitedly discussing. The facial types, whether oval or round, are always vacuous—we know them from the Bruges altar panel. The cheeks are wide, the large ears placed far from the close-set eyes.

96 Again, I have spotted no more than three pictures by the hand of the more talented, earlier painter whom I have dubbed the Master of the André Madonna, after a work in the Musée Jacquemart-André (187, Plate 189). In addition to this panel, there is a full-length Madonna with four angels, now in the collection of Baron H. Thyssen, from the Dr. E. Simon collection in Berlin (188, Plate 190); and a Madonna at half-length in private hands at Harburg (189, Plate 190).

We gain a favourable albeit rather one-sided impression from this small, compact group of wistful Madonnas. They look as though they were done by a descendant of Jan van Eyck, a legitimate heir, so to speak, who retained the virtues of the heroic age, but managed to combine them with the milder formal and stylistic taste of his own generation. There can be no doubt that he worked in Bruges, for the town's symbol, the steeple of Notre Dame, rises in the background of the standing Madonna in the Thyssen collection.

Grave and noble in expression, her heavy head inclined in half-face, the Virgin casts her eyes low. Her hair, held in place by a plain dark band, falls full and wide over her shoulders. The pure round sweep of the cheeks is emphasized, the chin arched out spherically. The nose is short in the child's face, the corners of the mouth turn down, and there is a precocious cast to the profoundly sorrowful features. A restorer has brightened them slightly in the Harburg picture. The tapering fingers and the long, bent-up thumb carry a hint of Provost, who was fond of giving his hands an insinuatingly graceful if not mannered configuration. In both of the half-length panels, a wall rises behind the Virgin, composed of foliage in one instance, in the other, the André Madonna, of houses and trees, forming an evocative element, firmly integrated with the figure in colour and form. The aim is not so much depth or distance, but rather to create a dark foil for the Virgin, a warm, shadowy colour harmony.

In the full-length picture, the Virgin stands within a richly modelled, arched gateway of considerable depth. White-robed angels holding musical instruments are seated on benches recessed into the sides. Two more angels supporting a crown hover above. A townscape occupies the bright background. The standing Virgin is descended from Jan van Eyck, whose *Virgin by the Fountain* in Antwerp displays similar drapery lines. Almost miniaturelike in its delicacy, the panel preserves all the grace of the 15th century and stands alone as a late flowering of Eyckian art.

The third of these masters, working around 1520, was a competent but unpretentious craftsman. Evidently he was a hard worker, for much output from his studio has come down to us. His name is derived from the place where one of his works has long been preserved. In the possession of the Brotherhood of the Holy Blood at Bruges is a triptych with a *Lamentation* (193, Plate 194), a work that does not show the artist's skill in a very favourable light[3]. A better impression is conveyed by another triptych, in the church of St. James at Bruges (195, Plates 197–199), showing the Virgin in the centrepiece with King Solomon, two prophets and two

3. Hulin's conjecture that this triptych was donated in 1519 by Jan van der Straeten does not seem to me correct, for the data in the evidence cited do not fit this work. Cf. *Le Beffroi*, Vol. 3, p. 344, Note 25.

sibyls. But for these triptychs done for Bruges altars to serve us as signposts, we would be scarcely inclined to place the master in this town. In terms of his types, he never cast off the spell of Quentin Massys, and his relationship to that dominant figure in Antwerp is not unlike that of the Master of the Mansi Magdalene.

In the altarpiece of the Brotherhood of the Holy Blood, St. John lifts the dead Saviour's arm into a horizontal position, echoing a motive from Quentin's Antwerp altarpiece. A man in a tall hat, gazing out of the picture to the front in alarm, shows the same provenance. We encounter the same female type in a number of Madonna paintings, for the most part of mediocre quality, and it too is clearly derived from Quentin's ideal. Nowhere do we find any connection with Gerard David, which might have been expected in Bruges. We are driven to conclude that the Master of St. Sang received his training in Antwerp, before moving on to Bruges.

When it comes to detailed stylistic studies, we tend to get bogged down. It is scarcely worth-while to take note of all the Madonnas, triptychs and other devotional pictures that issued from the workshop of the Master of St. Sang. Many of them are crude in execution, formal idiom and types. We rarely find donor portraits in his altarpieces, and their lack may be taken as a sign that he worked mainly for the market, probably in many cases the export market, and rarely received specific commissions.

A few of these pictures stand out from the great mass and are distinguished by comparatively careful workmanship. Examples are a Madonna with three angels in the Antwerp Museum (208, Plate 204), and a half-length Madonna that recently reached the Percy Strauss collection in New York (203, Plate 202).

The Antwerp panel combines one of Memling's compositional schemes with types in the style of Massys, in a manner characteristic of this master's mentality. The Virgin is seated at the centre. The child on her lap reaches one arm out stiffly towards a piece of fruit proffered him by an angel standing at the left. On the right are two angels with a prayer book. On the projecting capitals of each of the pillars on the right and left stand two nude children holding garlands, and above them on both sides are sculptural elements, showing the sacrifice of Abraham and the beheading of St. John the Baptist. All this is similar to Memling's Florentine Madonna panel. The ornamentation runs riot. The scrollwork on the capitals suggests cabbage leaves. In his drapery folds, the master seeks to capture the rhythm and melody of Quentin but all too often lapses into a pattern of harsh and brittle creases.

It is his weaknesses by which he is easiest recognized—certain recurrent faults, gaps in his knowledge of form. The child's extended arm resembles an overstuffed sausage. In many cases, an unmistakable mark is an excessively large ear, placed high up—it is almost a signature.

The half-length figure in the Strauss collection at New York carries a particularly strong infusion of Quentin's positive and effective qualities. The Bruges master may here have based himself on a drawing he had brought along from his days in the Antwerp studio. The shaft of the column, hewn from a material like agate, is almost worthy of Quentin, as is the head of the Virgin. The bold postures are also probably derived from Massys. The child reaches into the neckline of his mother's dress with his right arm, which covers his chest and neck. The contrast of light and dark is much cruder than in any of Quentin's works; but apart from this, other marks identify the author—the Virgin's large ear, emerging through her complex coiffure, framed in a pinned-back braid; braceletlike folds on the child's arm; and a certain smoothness of the flesh parts, which reflect the light almost like metal.

An excellent opportunity for appreciating the peculiarities of this master is
98 afforded by a triptych with a *Holy Family*, and with female saints on the shutters, that was ascribed to Massys when it was in the Weber collection (194, Plate 196). The painter struggled hard to invest the work with rather harsh surface effects. The head of the Virgin is quite as in the panel at New York. Joseph is clean-shaven, directly frontal, with heavy shadows—a dark trail that bisects the face next to the nose. The child's body displays painstaking indentations. The linen about the sleeves of the saints on the right shutter is marked by the same abundance of fabric, with harsh, papery lines, as are seen in the Bruges altarpieces. In the background landscape are blocks of dark foliage and bright, equally massive towers of rock.

The master took great pains in his drawing of the hands, without being always rewarded with success. His fingers are slackly parallel, and when he forces them into some kind of action or grasp, he seems to tie off the digits and emphasize the joints. Uncertainly striving to show his hands foreshortened or shifted in one aspect or another, he often seems to draw the finger contours at an angle to the axis of the palm; and there are many occasions when persistent flaws in the draughtsmanship of precisely this organ reveals his authorship. There are a few occasions when one senses him half-succeeding in imitating the noble, elegant, animated hands of Quentin Massys.

From the documentary evidence, the lists of names in the Antwerp guild, and our general knowledge of the historical circumstances, we are conditioned to expect that the mainstream of migration flowed from Bruges to Antwerp. Here we note that the direction was sometimes reversed, the forms of Massys gaining entry in Bruges.

Joachim Patenier

Patenier is accounted the earliest landscape painter. Dürer praises him as *den gut Landschaftsmaler*, possibly using that professional designation for the first time. It is true that Patenier, unlike any Netherlander before or beside him, sedulously cultivated the new genre. The outdoors as a valid pictorial theme on its own triumphed only in later centuries, and Patenier appears as a forerunner and pioneer and thus may be getting credit beyond his due. One early witness to his prestige is the Spaniard de Guevara[1], who in 1540 enumerated the three greatest Netherlandish painters as follows: *Johannes* (van Eyck); *Rugier* (Rogier); and *Patinier!*

1. Cf. wol. 1, p. 34.

A brilliant connoisseur once said that the best landscapes were done by painters who were not landscapists at all—Titian, Rubens, Rembrandt. A supplement to this proposition would be the statement that the art of landscape painting was established by Jan van Eyck, Dieric Bouts, Geertgen tot Sint Jans, Gerard David and Jerome Bosch, rather than by Joachim Patenier. The essential element in its genesis is the painter's viewpoint, his love for the outdoors aspect of the visible world, his sense of the sublimity of mood that may repose in the configurations of the countryside. How much of a picture is devoted to landscape and how much to the figures is quite immaterial. There is, as a matter of fact, no 'pure landscape' in all Patenier's œuvre. Like his fellows, he depicted religious or genre scenes. He departs from his predecessors in degree rather than kind, changing the proportionate scale. His figures become mere appurtenances. In terms of the pictorial theme, they are still the primary element, but in terms of space and form they take second place.

The causes of this transformation must be sought not so much in the painter's own imaginative world as in the needs and predilections of his time. What I mean to say is that it was not creative genius as such that forced new visions upon a generation. That generation itself called out for a shift in the centre of gravity, demanded a new type of painting.

If the Virgin begins to recede, giving more prominence to her spatial surroundings, this betokens a more highly secularized appreciation of painting, a rational striving for more natural contexts. The world was huge, man a mere grain of sand in it. Earth had begun to rivet the attention of scholars, explorers, travellers and poets—and it was expanding apace. In the 15th century, painters first conquered space, caused the lyrical tones of nature to sound forth. Now, early in the 16th century, the trend had reached the point where the new genre, nurtured in the bosom of ecclesiastical art, began to declare its independence. It found devotees of its own and provided a living for its practitioners. The incidents and figures that were fitted into the outdoors scene ultimately became no more than the occasion and pretext for representing the countryside as such.

In the case of St. Jerome mortifying his flesh in the wilderness, one first saw the scene and only then discovered the tiny figure lost and surrendered to the vastness of space. This primacy and dominion of the soil, with its teeming multitudes, was in accord with the growing knowledge of the physical world. In the 15th century, the countryside had been perceived as background, as a distant vision. Slowly, this visual approach was changing. It was not that the trees greatly increased in size, now that locale was gaining in pictorial importance. Rather, man modestly withdrew into the depth, retired to a more seemly distance. He was no longer the centre of things. Spatial depth and spacious skies aroused awe of the unseen divinity.

And, in awe of creation, one worshipped the Creator. Faith began to turn into the direction of pantheism.

Patenier became a free master in Antwerp in 1515, and he died there in 1524. He was born in Bouvignes—at least, this claim, put forward by Guicciardini, seems more plausible than van Mander's statement, which mentions Dinant. Everything van Mander tells us about Patenier must be regarded with suspicion, for van Mander quite evidently and mistakenly related data about Herri Patenier to the much older Joachim. Herri, who is very probably the painter we now call Herri met de Bles, became a master in 1535, as against Joachim's date of 1515. Van Mander wavered in respect of the latter date and fancied he improved matters by correcting 1515 to 1535. He gives Bouvignes as Herri met de Bles's birthplace, which Guicciardini puts at Dinant. Van Mander seems to have confused birthplaces as well as dates.

When Patenier came to Antwerp in 1515, he was presumably at least 35 years old, hence must have already been working elsewhere. Dürer drew his likeness in 1521, but the drawing is lost. Yet there can be no doubt that the engraving by Cort (A, Plate 254) in the well-known sequence of painter's portraits published in 1572 goes back to Dürer's drawing of 1521. In the portrait, the master looks to be a man of at least 40, which would fix the year of his birth at about 1480; but we have no idea at all where he worked before he came to Antwerp. Herri Patenier, appearing on the Antwerp scene in 1535, was presumably a nephew of Joachim's and certainly his follower in a stylistic sense. If Herri came from Dinant and Joachim from Bouvignes, a place close by, we are entitled to conjecture that there was a local or family tradition in respect of the appreciation of landscape. The region of Dinant is hilly, with a river course, and rich in bare rock formations of picturesque aspect. More than once in the history of landscape painting, we have occasion to note that the sight of mountainous country apparently stimulates the pictorial imagination to creative work. Joachim's origins, and possibly his training in Dinant, may have permanently turned his mind towards landscape.

What we possess of Patenier's work, he did for the most part in Antwerp, during the brief decade of his career there. It was only in such a town, eager for novelty, highly specialized in its art life, that a master himself so highly specialized could find reward and recognition. Only in Antwerp was the market large enough, the export trade at a sufficiently high volume, the taste of connoisseurs discriminating. Patenier, moreover, was able to serve as a collaborator, adding landscape backgrounds to compositions by other masters. Massys worked with him in this way. This is apparent in at least one case, the *Temptation of St. Anthony*, preserved in the Prado [54]. Patenier also seems to have joined hands with Joos van Cleve. At least, van Mander tells of a Madonna by Joos, to which Patenier had added a beautiful landscape[2].

2. Cf. Vol. IX, part I, p. 20.

When collaboration is incontestable in one case, it must be taken as possible in countless others. The connoisseur is under the obligation to consider that a single work may have two authors. The question whether the landscape portion was painted by Patenier has indeed been raised in respect of the works of many masters, just as one must ask before every work ascribed to Patenier whether the figures may not come from another hand.

We shall proceed from three pictures bearing signed inscriptions. A *Baptism of Christ*, in Vienna (221, Plate 216), a *Flight into Egypt*, in the Antwerp museum (231, Plate 220), and a *St. Jerome*, in Karlsruhe (239, Plate 228), all agree conspicuously in the form of the name displayed: *Opus Joachim D. Patinir* (in Vienna: *Patinier*). The panels in Antwerp and Karlsruhe are small and of little significance; but the *Baptism* with its comparatively large figures tells us a good deal. The signature testifies to our master's authorship—of the figures as well. It would be strange if he, who signed his work only in exceptional cases, should have done so on a painting that was but half his.

In the *Baptism*, a river bed winds away into the distance, through mountainous country. The beholder's eye falls on the mirror-smooth surface from a considerable height. Three-quarters of the picture area is taken up by the earth, the remaining quarter by the sky with its streaks of clouds. This was the way in which the masters of the 15th century saw landscape background. Patenier was also true to tradition in that he relinquished perspective and showed in normal, unforeshortened aspect rather than from above those elements of the picture that loom up vertically, such a rocks, trees and even figures, especially in the foreground and middleground. His ground plane is like a steeply inclined stage, on which the flats nevertheless stand bold upright—i.e. at an obtuse angle to the gradient.

The relation between figures and landscape is not much different from Gerard David's *Baptism of Christ*[3]. At the foremost level, Jesus is shown in the water up to his knees, while the Baptist kneels on the rocky bank, and is shown again in the middleground, preaching to his flock. The only element in David's panel that is missing here is the angel at the extreme foreground, holding Jesus's robe. Yet Patenier, without increasing the landscape elements in a quantitative sense, has nevertheless managed to make them a good deal more expressive. The landscape is what one remembers of Patenier's picture, while of David's it is the figures. A sense of dramatic tension emanates from Patenier's empty and inhospitable immensity, especially the clash between horizontal and vertical features. The bare, grey rock pinnacles, like petrified giants, carry an air of menace. Against such a background of cosmic solitude, the solemn baptismal scene gathers added symbolic meaning.

3. Cf. Vol. VI, part II, No. 161, Plate 167.

In no other place does Patenier appear in such towering splendour as in the Prado. His four masterpieces there harmonize so perfectly with the signed picture at Vienna that our view of him is rounded out into reassuring certainty. Every additional word seems superfluous to establish his authorship.

In one of the Madrid panels (235, Plates 224, 225), the Virgin is seated on a knoll in the ground at the centre foreground, her relation to the landscape and picture area much the same as that of the figure of Christ in the Vienna painting (221, Plate 216). The figure of the Virgin is on the large side, with her white robe quite prominent. Nevertheless, she could be eliminated, without destroying the picture's

integrity. Its theme is *Rest on the Flight into Egypt.* To the extreme fore, basket, staff, knotted bundle and flask ostentatiously document the journey. Joseph and the ass have been moved far into the distance, at a considerable interval from each other. We are again reminded of Gerard David, who used pictorial elements and situations in similar fashion. But Patenier the 'landscape painter' does not adapt
 his format vertically to the human figure. He follows the horizontal configuration of the ground into breadth. He has overcome any fear of emptiness. Reeds, shrubs, thorny stems that resemble trip wires, tree roots and pieces of rock—all these he welcomes as foreground elements of equal value with the human figure. To the extreme fore rises an ivy-grown tree with this foliage, its crown cut off at the top by the frame.

There is a friendly air to the parklike countryside with its rich articulation. It invites and envelops us. The rough mountains have receded and loom only in the far distance. The Holy Family has found a safe resting-place. The harsh, sharp-edged rocks may express an ascetic gravity, a deathlike rigour, but the deep-green, succulent trees in their mid-summer opulence speak of growth and idyllic peace. Their foliage belongs to the Virgin, as rocks belong to the Baptist and St. Jerome, and water to St. Christopher.

The earth gives an impression of solidity and stability, for the key contours run approximately parallel to the horizon, while hills, trees and houses are seen in frontal view. The broad expanses of land are neither tilled nor cropped. Every segment stands immutably in its proper place, part of an organic integration of soil, plants and buildings.

Unlike the mere decorator, Patenier does not abhor a vacuum. His control of perspective in line and space is sovereign, as he proclaims earth's grandeur and variety. For him, an area between two objects, even though pervaded only by the empty air, is a full-fledged pictorial element. Many of his contemporaries looked upon the countryside as though it were a carpet, densely and evenly woven of houses, trees and paths. Their fussy accumulations lack the sonorous ring that sounds in greater or lesser degree from every one of Patenier's creations.

Preserved in the Prado is a *Temptation of St. Anthony* with the figures from Quentin's hand[4]—the horizon lies at an unusually high level in this picture—and further a *St. Jerome* (240, Plates 230, 231) and a *River Styx* (253, Plate 242). Lastly, a *St. Christopher*, in the Escorial (246, Plates 235-237), is among the masterpieces by Patenier preserved in Spain.

4. Cf. Vol. VII, No. 31, Pl. 35.

His unique vision of the underworld (253, Plate 242) is vertically divided into three segments. At the left is the shore of paradise, at the right, hell, and in the middle, the wide, sluggish stream, reaching from the lower edge to the horizon, its unfathomable depth conveyed solely by colour tints and nuances of light. In mid-stream is Charon with his boat, which holds a tiny nude figure—a human soul. It is a curious mixture of pagan and Christian mythology—Hades combined with hell and paradise. The tranquillity peculiar to all of the master's compositions here rises to the level of sublime desolation. The line of the horizon, across the water, lies parallel to the upper edge of the picture, and rocky and wooded headlands, bright or dark, project alternately into the river.

Buildings constructed in perspective, tend to speak a clear language, especially a tiled floor. On the other hand, landscapes, even when rendered in perfect perspective, fail to give a clear answer to the question in what measure extension is determined by 'local form'—using this term by analogy with 'local colour'—or by its relation to the beholder's point of vantage. We do not actually know the 'local form'—i.e. we do not know how high is this hill as such, how wide that valley. Only a water level, looming all the way to the horizon as a plane surface, speaks unequivocally, leaves no doubt as to the point from which the view strikes it. To Patenier, water was a regulator, a geometrical point of reference, and he was fond of carrying it through all the levels of his pictures. The pure line of the horizon he lays bare as a unifying pictorial axis, but unlike mountain ranges, the waterline does not serve to terminate the space. It merely indicates how far the eye reaches. Imagination tends to glide beyond it, into the distance.

Descriptive hints of hell are given in the *River Styx*—a turretlike portal with fire and brimstone and a monstrous creature as gatekeeper. Here Patenier was drawing on common resources. None but Jerome Bosch knew his way about hell, and every Netherlander stuck to Bosch's delineation. But Patenier respected the perfection of wholesome organic growth. Fantasy went against his grain, as did every kind of exaggeration, every adulteration or distortion of what is seen. In contrast to Bosch, he was alert and sensible, stuck close to the truth. Yet the connection between Patenier and Bosch is sensed all the more deeply as one enters into the minds of the two masters. In construction and conception of the countryside, Bosch anticipated the younger master in many respects. Patenier, however, exploited and cultivated professionally what his inspired predecessor had scattered casually and lavishly in the backgrounds of his panels. Bosch died in 1516, only a year after Patenier had settled in Antwerp; yet there was ample occasion to study the art of Bosch in Antwerp. His influence on landscape representation, as it began to emerge in Antwerp around 1515, can be felt elsewhere too—for example, in the works of the master whom we have good reason to name Jan de Cock. What Bosch awakened was the awe of wide-open spaces, the multiple aspects of plant life[5].

5. Cf, Vol. v, p. 64.

Patenier depicted St. Christopher more than once. Among the versions that have come down to us are one in the Escorial (246, Plates 235-237), another presently in the possession of a Berlin art dealer (247, Plate 239), and a third, in the Chiaramonte Bordonaro collection at Palermo (248, Plate 239), known to me only from a poor reproduction. Bosch too painted St. Christopher more than once. A large panel showing the sainted giant and bearing Bosch's authentic signature is currently on the Berlin art market [55]. Comparison of this panel, tall and narrow in the Gothic manner, with the versions Patenier spread out horizontally, as was his wont, throws a surprisingly sharp light on the relation between the two masters. Patenier's composition contains traits that are explained neither by tradition nor by his personal imagination, but that are borrowed from Bosch, or at least stimulated by him. He shows a bewitched region, bare, heavily populated, with dead trees, full of menace and curious goings-on—for example, a hermit has built his refuge in a tree top. The whole countryside has been given a demoniac aspect, in the spirit of Bosch. Sensible and straightforward by nature, the master here helped himself liberally to romantic seasoning.

It is not merely that Patenier borrowed a few odd motives from Bosch's inexhaustible spectral world; when we carry comparison farther, we find he also followed Bosch in his construction of distant landscape elements, pointed promontaries, shadowy thickets along the banks. Those aspects in which Patenier departed from Bosch, moreover, become clear. Patenier observed landscapes conscientiously, favouring no particular distance. He elaborated his plant life in the foreground with scientific precision, his rocks with similar surgical detachment. In Bosch's pictures, on the other hand, the foreground, reserved to the figures, rises up like a bare wall. Patenier's creatures are unmistakably real, while Bosch's are symbolic and charged with meaning. Patenier never divides his landscapes into compartments, nor does he join his various grounds by shifting masses obliquely. He escalates his land into steps with many horizontal alternations of light and dark, of forests ranges and water courses, fading towards the horizon, the striped effect often being carried over into the cloud formations.

Saints often gave this painter occasion to paint their homelands, and St. Jerome, already a favoured object of devotion at the time, was bound to be particularly welcome. We do indeed have numerous panels in the style of Patenier, showing the aged ascetic down front, yet tiny and as though lost. The saint's ramshackle shelter is a lean-to hut perched against steep rocks. He is shown praying, chastising himself, or nursing the lion. Pre-eminent among the *St. Jerome* panels we may with assurance regards as Patenier's work is the one in the Prado (240, Plates 230, 231), while the large and unusually broad one donated to the Louvre (245, Plate 238) a few years ago is of about equal merit, as is a small panel recently acquired (together with a pendant, 251, Plate 232) on the Munich art market (243 b, Plate 232) for a private collection in Germany. There is a slightly inferior replica of the Louvre picture in the Cà d'Oro in Venice (245 a, Plate 238). Patenier repeated this third composition several times, with only minor changes. A left half of it is in the Oppenheim collection at London (243 a, Plate 233). A full replica, on the Munich art market in 1916, is now in the Elberfeld museum (243, Plate 232).

Craggy rocks rise steeply from the plain, while the background on the other side is filled with bodies of water, wooded and hilly tongues of land, and houses. The rocky peaks jutting up abruptly in the middleground rise almost to the top edge of the picture. The horizontal lines of the plain clash with the vertical lines of the mountain range.

The elemental power of nature that piled up these rocks skywards is driven home all the more impressively by the way the counter-pressure is successfully met, as expressed in the obliqueness and inclination of the rock formations. These great and looming mountains seem almost to have been bent back at the top. They suggest huge buildings, with columns, flying buttresses and arches; and by suggesting man's handiwork, they express aspiration and willpower—and also supplications offered to heaven.

What lends Patenier's countryside such an air of satisfying completeness is that it reaches out in all three dimensions. The eye pushes on into the distance, soars proudly upwards, glides unhindered broadside. This is precisely what distinguishes the master from his predecessors and contemporaries. He applies his creative powers fairly and neutrally, so to speak. He shows that space is infinite in every direction, evenly filled out everywhere. His sense of harmony is one of Patenier's personal virtues; and this is seen with particular clarity in the half-width fragment in the Oppenheimer collection. Here the mountains loom up within an almost square format, leaving an oppressive and disquieting impression. The resolution of dramatic tension is absent.

In the *St. Jerome* panels, a monastery is placed at an intermediate altitude. It is fondly elaborated, with understanding for the scope of architecture, rather than 'picturesquely' approximated to chance organic form in the Boschian manner. Providing a scale of reference for its inhospitable natural setting, the pious settlement hurls defiance at the wilderness.

The same solidly constructed complex of buildings—church façade, towers and habitations—is seen in the panels at Madrid and Paris, with only minor shifts and modifications. The structures stand firm and almost windowless, in the Romanesque rather than the Gothic style, organized along predominantly horizontal lines.

Among Patenier's virtues is a sense of obligation to serve as a dependable guide and knowledgeable scout to the broad, richly articulated terrain he spreads out before us. He is as precise as might be a geographer or geologist. Nothing is fudged or blurred.

When one comes down to it, it does not really matter whether a hill or a tree has this size and form or that. Landscape representation, in consequence, is anything but a school of fidelity. In the course of the 16th century, painters soon took advantage of the opportunity for letting themselves go, without possibility of control. Patenier, however, never lets up, is never vague or arbitrary.

His palette of local colour is limited, but varied in many nuances. To the fore the brownish tones are warm, with light grey rocks. Saturated greens and many shades of distant blue combine into luminous harmony. Pure pigments, applied in the manner of a glaze, are systematically used to create the illusion of aerial space—transparent, tinted hazes and mirror-smooth water surfaces. Patenier's palette holds one blue for distances of a quarter-mile, and another for distances of half a mile.

We get into many a quandary from the ever-present chance that Patenier's paintings may include figures by another hand, or that paintings by other masters may carry landscapes by Patenier. Both as a draughtsman and a painter, Patenier never felt sure of himself when it came to the human body. His weakness in this area is confirmed by a well-known passage in Dürer's travel diary. Dürer gave the landscape painter what was either one sheet with four figures of St. Christopher, or four drawings, each of a single figure[6].

Patenier solicited and accepted this gift with the intention of enriching his compositions with the German's pictorial ideas. The figure in his panel in the Escorial (246, Plates 235-237) probably goes back to one of Dürer's models. Panofsky has called attention to the relation between this figure and a corresponding one, reversed, in Dürer's engraving B. 51 (1521)[7]. Patenier's source, however, was more likely one of Dürer's drawings rather than the engraving. We thus would gain a date, after 1521, for this painting.

Looking at any picture by Patenier, one must consider three possibilities: He may have invented and painted the figures himself; he may have done them after models by others; and, lastly, he may have had someone else paint them for him.

The rather large human figures in the *Baptism of Christ* at Vienna (221, Plate 216)

6. *Dürers Schriftlicher Nachlass...* ed. by Dr. K. Lange and Dr. F. Fuhse, Halle, 1893, p. 166.

7. *Zeitschrift für Bildende Kunst*, 1928, p. 182. Cf. also J. Held, *Dürers Wirkung auf die Niederländische Kunst seiner Zeit*, The Hague, 1931, p. 67.

and the Madonna panel at Madrid (235, Plates 224, 225) agree in formal idiom. Their drawing is shown to be by a competent disciple of Quentin, one not given to taking unnecessary risks, taking over forms with care and good sense, offering no more than is required for spare and clear-cut presentation. We do indeed learn that Patenier was on close terms with Massys. After his death, Massys is named as

one of the guardians of his orphaned daughters. It was Patenier who introduced Dürer into Quentin's home; and we may surmise that Quentin, older than Patenier and his intellectual superior, entertained a patronizing friendship for the landscape painter. Patenier looked up to Massys, as a craftsman in figure-drawing; and it is very likely that he felt no compunction in taking advantage of his personal connection with the master he revered, by borrowing forms and motives from him.

I have a vivid recollection of the triptych in the Kaufmann collection (218, Plates 208-210), badly damaged by fire in 1904, and there are surviving photographs, taken before this disaster. It contains figures in the foreground, middleground and background and has a wholly convincing air of unity. Both the figures and the landscape look as though they were done by the same hand. In the centre, the Virgin, with the child, is seated in the foreground, on a rise in the ground, her figure almost half as high as the picture. Her cloak falls away widely on either side. At the right, beside the pyramid-shaped main figure, is the travel gear, including a straw hamper that recurs in the same place and similar form in the Madonna panels at Madrid (235, Plates 224, 225) and Berlin (237, Plates 226, 227), in the Deutsches Museum. In the middleground, Joseph kneels at a well to draw water. Behind him is the grazing ass. Farther back on the right is a field, with one peasant working a plough and another a harrow, while a third one reaps the ripe grain. Soldiers are shown, in pursuit of the infant Jesus, and far back, in the village square, the Slaughter of the Innocents is seen. The peopling of the scene in depth is quite as in the Madrid panel, although not a single motive is copied. From the tiniest figures, inseparably tied to the locale, the eye moves step by step forward, sliding over the intermediate figures to the dominant figure of the Virgin in the foreground. The transition is smooth. There are no sharp dividing lines, no stylistic jumps.

The same thing is true of the shutters of the Kaufmann triptych. On the left is St. John the Baptist, on the right Pope Cornelius, dignified albeit somewhat stodgy upright figures, occupying about two-thirds of the picture's height. In type and turn of head, the rather youthful St. John resembles his counterpart in the Vienna *Baptism of Christ* (221, Plate 216). Feet and hands are shaped the same way. The fall of the drapery differs slightly—it is busier, harsher and stiffer in the triptych. In the Vienna picture, as in the Madrid Madonna (235, Plates 224, 225) and the *St. Christopher* in the Escorial (246, Plates 235-237), the fabric motives, while economical, have a curving sweep. Occasionally they seem almost to balloon and swirl away into space. We might conclude, from these small differences, that the triptych was painted a bit earlier than the other works considered in this context; or we may prefer the theory that Patenier helped himself to his felicitously harmonious figures by the use of model drawings from Quentin's studio; but in any event, we now recognize the style of Patenier the figure painter as a reasonably consistent feature of his work.

When connoisseurs are challenged to determine Patenier's possible authorship of a picture, they will, first of all, examine its landscape aspects, for they will look for the master's peculiarities to be more marked there than in the figure-work. Yet there are a few instances in which pictures are identifiable as his work precisely from the head shapes, the drapery, the postures. The most extraordinary case is a *Crucifixion* (224, Plate 217) I came upon several years ago in the possession of a Munich art dealer—it is now in the Schlayer collection in Madrid. All the 15th and 16th century masters painted Calvaries, and each necessarily impressed his own character on the locale, the mount on which the crosses rise, the city in the distance. Patenier might have been expected to detail his physical setting very explicitly, but this is precisely what he did not do. Apparently he was mindful of the tradition that the skies darkened at the Saviour's death, plunging the land into almost complete night. Except for a small area on the right, where some buildings shine forth glaringly, virtually all landscape elements are extinguished. Yet even with this paradoxical renunciation of his customary bag of tricks, Patenier the landscape painter did not really focus on his figures, but based himself on the atmospheric ambiance, on the peculiar lighting. His figures stand like helpless, insignificant puppets before a dark wall.

The British collector J. P. Heseltine sent a relatively large Madonna at half-length (227, Plate 219) to Bruges in 1902, with an attribution to Patenier that has not been generally accepted. The picture, by the way, has more recently been on the market in Amsterdam. In my opinion, it has many features characteristic of the master—the quiet, gently curving but mainly horizontal parallels of hills and tree lines, the rhythmical alternation of light and dark, the body of water on the horizon, the level field, the clouded sky, the single, large tree cut off by the frame; then, too, the Virgin with her vacant, oval face and lofty brow, the child, reminiscent of Massys, and above all the arching, crushed fabric of the Virgin's mantle.

Patenier is said to have had a hand in the works of many other masters, but sometimes the assertion is put forward with little conviction. Among those mentioned are Quentin Massys, the Master of the Mansi Magdalene, Joos van Cleve, Adriaen Isenbrant, and the Master of the Female Half-Lengths. In the older literature, Gerard David and Bernart van Orley are also named in this connection, almost certainly in error.

In respect of Massys, the question must be taken seriously but is hard to answer. An effort is certainly in order to distinguish his style of landscape painting from that of Patenier. Massys had already achieved a deep understanding of the mood and expressiveness of backgrounds, before his relationship with Patenier began—in the Antwerp *St. Christopher*, for example. A regular process of exchange between the studios of Quentin and Patenier is likely for the period between 1515 and 1524. But even when we find landscapes in certain of Quentin's paintings that are very definitively constructed along Patenier's lines—like the *Crucifixion* in the Liechtenstein Gallery at Vienna or the altar shutters in the Carstanjen collection—we are reluctant to jump to the conclusion that Patenier intervened directly. Massys may very well have approximated the specialist's style; or his assistants and students may have availed themselves of schemes developed by Patenier. Around 1540, Cornelis Massys, Quentin's son, was competently imitating Patenier's landscape

forms, especially in drawings. The Madonna in the Raczynsky collection at Poznan is a special case. Its horizon is placed conspicuously high, unlike any of Quentin's other compositions; and the almost pedantically horizontal arrangement of the plain, seen in geographical perspective, is so utterly at odds with the figure group that I feel certain a landscape painter collaborated—and who else could it have been
108 but Patenier?

The more we cast about within the Antwerp and Bruges output, the more wide-spread and authoritative Patenier's system seems to have been. The Master of the Mansi Magdalene[8], a faithful follower of Massys in his figures, imitated Patenier quite successfully in his backgrounds. He managed to extract dramatic effects from strong contrasts of light and dark at dusk, and he proves himself a better hand at landscape than at figures.

8. Cf. Vol. VII, pp. 45-47.

I have already speculated on Patenier's relationship to Joos van Cleve[9]. The backgrounds in Joos's altarpieces and devotional paintings are essentially of the same kind and remind one more or less of Patenier.

9. Cf. Vol. IX, Part I, p. 20.

It is possible to single out an occasional work—which has indeed been done—and point to it as an example of collaboration between the two masters. Such was Justi's opinion of the wide panel in Brussels, showing the Virgin giving suck (49, Plate 63). The travel gear in the right foreground—plaited pannier, staff and bundle, identical objects placed entirely similarly in three Pateniers—would seem to support this conjecture. Yet we find the basket in paintings by Gerard David and Adriaen Isenbrant as well. The landscape coincides in many details with Patenier's, in the picture that has gone from the Kaufmann and Simon collections to Schloss Rohoncz (232, Plate 221). Nor is there any dearth of other panels with figures by Joos and landscapes seemingly bearing Patenier's mark, such as the wide *Virgin with St. Dominic* in the Louvre (50, Plate 64) and the *St. Jerome* from the Holzapfel collection (41, Plate 58). In the Paris picture, the Virgin is seated on a rock ledge in a curious way. It looks as though a configuration set by one painter gave the other a good deal of trouble. The one who did the wide bench probably envisaged a Virgin seated upon it frontally. When Joos proceeded to compose mother and child in side-view, he had to settle for a masculine straddle, not only inappropriate but in view of the robe quite impossible. Such observations support the idea of collaboration, of course. An exchange of pictorial motives between the workshops of Patenier and Joos seems all the more probable since figures of the Virgin invented by Joos occur in copies in landscapes by Patenier and his followers.

There is not a single painting by Joos van Cleve in which one can find landscape elements fundamentally different from Patenier's scheme. Joos continued to work for some 16 years after Patenier's death, yet there is no faltering. One cannot say that, with Patenier gone, the landscapes in Joos's paintings underwent a radical change. The likelihood is that Joos, with his characteristic adaptability, simply worked very much like Patenier, who may have actually helped out in person on a few occasions, soon after 1515. The stronger the effect of Joos's backgrounds, the more closely do they seem related to Patenier's style. Yet, on average, they are busier, with many points of light, contain more elements, are more evenly strewn with trees and houses.

The relationship of the Master of the Female Half-Lengths to Patenier is similar to that of Joos van Cleve—indicating, by the way, that Antwerp was the scene where the former worked. He was an uncommonly productive artist. It is quite plain that he ran a kind of factory, for a large number of panels, equal in appearance and merit, have accumulated, not merely Magdalenes, but half-length Madonnas and devotional works on other themes. Landscape backgrounds are rare in these pictures. When they do appear, they are more or less plainly reminiscent of Patenier —with a single exception. A Madonna [56] in the collection of Count d'Ursel at Bruges[10] startles with a very different landscape, boldly extending into the distance and presumably added by a younger master. It is a fact that the Master of the Female Half-Lengths painted shoddy merchandise for the market, for export, in soulless routine. Would Patenier have condescended to take part in such a scheme?

10. Reproduced in *Meisterwerke der Niederländischen Malerei des* XV. *und* XVI. *Jahrhunderts auf der Ausstellung zu Brügge 1902*, ed. by Max J. Friedländer, Bruckmann, Munich, 1903, Pl. 79.

A Madonna in Copenhagen [57] and the *St. John on Patmos* in the London National Gallery [58] have sometimes been considered the common work of these two painters. Reviewing the total œuvre of the nameless master, I distrust these observations. In my view, he is more a clever imitator of Patenier. I hold a similar view of the Master of the Parrot, who occasionally adds dusky, mood-charged landscape backgrounds to his Madonnas—e.g. the picture in the Feist collection, Berlin-Wannsee [59].

Quite different is the relationship with Patenier of Adriaen Isenbrant—or the master whom we have grown accustomed to call by that name. This is a more complex question. In the first place, Isenbrant worked in Bruges rather than Antwerp, and then, his landscapes are very variable. They really proceed from Gerard David, as does his whole art. In some of his pictures, he displays an easily recognized peculiarity. His weakly textured rocks, like arrowheads in form, look as though they had dropped from the sky and embedded themselves in the soil at an angle.

Yet there are pictures by him with landscapes reminding one remarkably of Patenier. A *Flight into Egypt* from the Thiem collection [60] does so to such a degree that I have, in this case, seriously considered the possibility of his collaboration. The town in the background, however, is enlivened with many dots of light, and it is busier than is Patenier's wont. Another *Flight into Egypt* in the Vienna Staatsgalerie [61] couples figures by Isenbrant with a landscape in which there is so much nature lore and keen observation in the foreground, especially in the way the stratified rock is elaborated, that Patenier's collaboration also becomes probable.

The differences in the panels that came from Isenbrant's busy workshop are explained by the employment of pupils and assistants. When we examine his very large accumulated œuvre, we necessarily conclude that discipline in his studio was not precisely rigorous. Apparently the master thought the landscape the least important part of a picture and slackened the reins for his assistants, when it came to such backgrounds. One or more of his pupils may have had a good grasp of Patenier's style and used it skilfully.

When we, lastly, find occasional Patenier-like backgrounds among the paintings of Ambrose Benson, we become fully converted to the view that this scheme was part and parcel of Bruges art life. It is at least a possibility that one of Patenier's disciples worked as a specialist in Bruges, taking a hand in the factory output of Isenbrant and Benson.

The net result of this survey is to increase our scepticism in respect of Patenier's œuvre. Apparently it was easy to follow in his footsteps, and more than one master succeeded in imitating him. We must be all the more severe and critical in delimiting his own achievement.

Around 1520, the countryside was depicted in Antwerp with curious uniformity,
110 almost monotony. Patenier was by no means a creative pioneer. He was a specialist of solid and conscientious craftmanship, gaining widespread acceptance for a way of landscape painting rooted in the work of Gerard David and Jerome Bosch. From Jan van Eyck to Pieter Bruegel, the masters who were independent observers of nature, fond of the countryside, were all Dutchmen, whether in the narrower or broader sense. The master from Bouvignes merely drew the proper conclusions from the work of others. It was Gerard David who erected the wood, the dark green wall of foliage as a mood-charged foil behind his figures, lending support and significance to the middleground. It was Jerome Bosch who invested the distance and the barren plains with pathos. We are reminded of the curious circumstance that David became a master in Antwerp in 1515, the same year as Patenier. Influences from Bruges may have reached Antwerp even earlier. Perhaps Patenier was temporarily in Bruges before 1515, as perhaps was Joos van Cleve before 1511.

We cannot really be surprised to find—in masters who worked in Antwerp before 1515, like the so-called Master of Hoogstraeten—landscape backgrounds related to those of Patenier. It is entirely reasonable that the younger artists should have so readily taken to an approach so well thought-out, so natural and organic, so much in keeping with the spirit of the time. This was the way the countryside looked, it was then widely believed; and the way Patenier showed it was the 'beautiful' way. The time had arrived for 'showpiece' pictures. As the human body, with all its parts and limbs, was a satisfying whole, so the earth with all she bore was a worthy object of contemplation—with her mountains, fields, plains, rivers, trees and houses. The distinguishing feature of the land was its size, and to take in its size, one had to look down upon it from above.

Patenier's success stems not least from the fact that he was something of an architect and something of a cartographer, choosing a vantage-point and directing the eye in such a way that the landscape perceived appeared as a complete unit.

When painters first represented divinity in human form, pictures were limited to one or more figures. Including the countryside meant that a piece of infinity was being added. Patenier, the first landscape painter, endeavoured to invest the views he showed with the qualities of totality. One feels in him a longing to survey the whole globe.

Patenier may have taken over as his own the achievements of Jerome Bosch and Gerard David and blended them. But it is his own original achievement to have put together the elements of space in a thoughtful way. His work was orderly, subject to rules, which means that it could be conveyed to others, learned, and this won it wide influence, both in place and in time.

The Catalogues

121. (Plates 137-139) *Altarpiece with Shutters, The Virgin Enthroned,* with Sts. Bernard and Benedict: on the shutters, the donor with St. John the Baptist, the donatrix with St. Barbara (?); verso, an old man holding a skull (symbolizing vanity, as in the panel in the municipal museum, Bruges, No. 126, below). Windsor Castle (rounded at the top). • Now in the Royal Collections, Hampton Court, Inv. No. 1419; 75 × 56.5—76 × 23.5 cm.

122. (Plates 140, 141) *Virgin and Child,* in half-length. On the shutters, *St. John the Evangelist* and *The Magdalene,* full-length. Rijksmuseum, Amsterdam, No. 1923b (44 × 31—52 × 15). From the C. Hoogendijk collection. The shutters display Provost's style more clearly than the centrepiece. • On loan to the Koninklijk Kabinet van Schilderijen, Mauritshuis, The Hague, No. 783; 44 × 30.5—50 × 14.5 cm.

123. (Plates 142, 143) *Altarpiece with Shutters, The Virgin Enthroned on the Altar,* with the two Johns, a pope and a donor family: left, *St. Sebastian*; right, *St. Christopher*; verso, Sts. Peter and Paul, in grisaille. Lisbon museum. • Inv. No. 697; 154.5 × 142.5—62.5 cm.

124. (Plates 144, 145) *Altarpiece with Shutters, The Adoration of the Magi*: left, *The Annunciation*; right, *The Nativity.* Art market, London (Douglas, 1912). • Now in the National Trust, Stourhead, Wiltshire, 85,5 × 71—30 cm.

125. (Plate 146) *Altarpiece with Shutters, The Adoration of the Magi*: on the shutters, *St. James the Pilgrim, St. Sebastian.* Art market, Paris (Sedelmeyer, 1906, 27 × 19—7.5). From the Westmacott collection, London. • Now in the Leopold Ruzicka-Stiftung, Kunsthaus, Zurich.

126. (Plate 147) Diptych, *Christ Carrying the Cross,* bust-length; *A Monk-Donor.* Bruges, hospital museum (35 × 25.5). Shown in Bruges in 1902, No. 189. Dated 1522 on the original frame. On the verso of the portrait, a skull in a niche.

127. (Plates 148, 149) *Three Altarpiece Panels, The Annunciation* (art market, Berlin); *The Nativity* (private ownership, New York, 1931); *Christ Appearing to His Mother* (private ownership, Paris). These three small panels were apparently parts of an altarpiece from the master's early period. • *The Annunciation* now in the Museum Boymans-van Beuningen, Rotterdam, Inv. No. 2642; 34 × 19 cm; *The Nativity* in 1941 in an English private collection. Present location unknown, 27,5 × 17 cm; *Christ appearing to his Mother,* Present location unknown 1621.

128. (Plate 150) *A Pair of Altarpiece Shutters, St. Jerome, St. John the Baptist.* Pinacoteca, Parma, Nos. 365, 376 (about 60 × 20). • 76.5 × 26 cm each.

129. (Plate 151) *A Pair of Altarpiece Shutters, A Prophet* (Prado, Madrid, No. 1296, 123 × 45); *A Sibyl* (Louvre, Paris, No. 2202C, 80 × 47, from the Lelong collection (1902)); verso, in grisaille, a female saint with a monstrance. Severely cropped at the bottom. • Inv. No. R. F. 1472 in the Musée du Louvre, Paris [63].

130. (Plate 155) *A Pair of Altarpiece Shutters, The Shepherds*; *Two Women* (the lost centrepiece carried a *Nativity*). Collection of Prince Czartoryski, Goluchov, Poland. Not in a perfect state of preservation. • Present location unknown.

131. (Plate 155) *A Pair of Altarpiece Shutters*, St. Catherine; a female saint holding a book and a palm frond. Both in half-length. Art market, Berlin (Perls, 1929, 75 × 24 each). • Now in the Mrs. J. van Stolk-Carp collection, Wassenaar, (Netherlands).

132. (Plates 152, 153) *A Pair of Altarpiece Shutters*, a donor with an episcopal saint [64]; a donatrix with St. Godelieve. Municipal museum, Bruges, Nos. 32, 33 (118 × 78 each). Shown in Bruges in 1902, No. 109. Rectos of the shutters listed next. • Inv. Nos. 216, 217; 120.5 × 78 cm and 120 × 79 cm.

133. (Plate 154) *A Pair of Altarpiece Shutters, Death and the Miser.* Municipal museum, Bruges, No. 39 (118 × 78 each). Very likely the versos of the shutters listed as No. 132, above. Shown in Bruges in 1902, No. 157. The inscription on the slip of paper held by the miser begins: *Ic. Jan Lanckaert* ... A similar scene appears on the versos [65] of the Windsor altarpiece, No. 121, above. • Inv. No. 218; 119.7 × 78.9 cm and 119.8 × 78.7 cm.

134. (Plates 158, 159) *A Pair of Altarpiece Shutters*, the donor with St. Andrew; the donatrix with St. Catherine; verso (separated), *The Annunciation*, in grisaille. Johnson collection, Philadelphia, Catalogue II, No. 355 (55.5 × 20 each, curved at the top). From the Somzée collection, Brussels. • 59 × 21.9 cm each.

135. (Plates 156, 157) *A Pair of Altarpiece Shutters, The Legend of St. Catherine* (see p. 88): *The Disputation of the Saint* (Rotterdam museum, 107 × 70); *The Beheading of the Saint* (Antwerp museum, No. 838, 94 × 68); verso, *St. Barbara.* Apparently somewhat cropped in the vertical dimension. • The Rotterdam panel, Inv. No. 1682.

136. (Plate 158) *A Pair of Altarpiece Shutters, St. John the Baptist, A Sainted Monk with a Star in his Hand* [66]. Art market, Amsterdam (Goudstikker, 1930, 61 × 19 each). From the Vieweg collection, Brunswick. • Now in the Rijksmuseum Twenthe, Enschede, 62 × 20.5 cm.

137. (Plates 160, 161). *A Pair of Altarpiece Shutters, St. Peter, St. Elizabeth*, in half-

length. Hospital, Genoa. • Now in the Palazzo Bianco, on loan from the Civil Hospital, 139 × 90 cm each.

138. (Plates 162, 163) *Three Altarpiece Panels, The Scourging of Christ, Christ on the Cross, The Lamentation.* Collection of Freiherr von Tucher, Munich. From the early period. • Now in the St. Louis Art Museum, St. Louis, Mo., Acc. Nos. 73 : 50, 74 : 50, 75 : 50; 27.3 × 20.9 cm each [166a].

139. (Plate 164) *Abraham and the Angel,* who foretells the birth of his son. Collection of Countess Durrieu, Paris, present whereabouts unknown (78 × 58). Shown in Paris in the *Primitifs Français* show, 1904, No. 136.

140. (Plate 165) *The Annunciation.* Hospital, Genoa (200 × 155). • Now in the Palazzo Bianco, on loan from the Civil Hospital, 258 × 202 cm.

141. (Plate 164) *The Annunciation.* Art market, Berlin (P. Cassirer). From the collection of Baron Thüngen, Rossbach castle, Franconia. Done at a rather early period. • Now in the Sir B. S. Barlow collection, Britain, 67 × 63 cm.

142. (Plate 164) *The Nativity.* Collection of Viscount Bearsted, London (71 × 30). From the collection of Lord Northesk. • Upton House, National Trust, Banbury, Cat. No. 165; 70.4 × 31.4 cm.

143. (Plate 166) *The Nativity.* Art market, Amsterdam (Goudstikker, 1920, 48 × 37). From the master's middle period, in part after Gerard David's Budapest panel. • Now in the Mrs. H. A. Wetzlar collection, Amsterdam; 51.5 × 38.7 cm.

144. (Plate 166) *The Adoration of the Magi.* Gemäldegalerie, Berlin, No. 551B (86 × 69). Overcleaned in places. About 1505. • Now in the Gemäldegalerie der Staatlichen Museen, Berlin-Dahlem.

145. *The Adoration of the Magi.* Private ownership, Madrid. From the early period. • Present location unknown.

146. (Plate 166) *The Baptism of Christ.* Convent, Guadalupe (rounded at the top). I have never seen the original and am judging only by a small reproduction.

147. (Plate 167) *Christ Carrying the Cross.* C. Stoop auction, Berlin, 1930. Sharply overcleaned in parts. • Auctioned 26th November 1970 at Lempertz, Cologne, No. 194; 71.5 × 53 cm.

148. (Plate 167) *Christ on the Cross.* Bondy collection, Vienna (32.5 × 26). Formerly in the Felix collection, Leipzig. From the early period. • Present location unknown.

149. *The Lamentation.* Traumann collection, Madrid, present whereabouts unknown. From the early period.

150. (Plate 167) *The Lamentation.* Schevitch auction, Paris, 1906, No. 19 (34 × 26). From the early period. • Present location unknown.

151. (Plate 167) *The Lamentation.* Collection of Dr. Boveri, Zurich (von Nemes auction, 1931, 80 × 58). Done at a rather early stage.

152. (Plate 168) *The Lamentation.* Art market, London (Knoedler, 1930, 42 × 33). From the Ferroni collection, Rome, the von Back collection, Szegedin, the Hauth collection, Düsseldorf. From the master's middle period. • Now in the Sterling and Francine Clark Art Institute, Williamstown, Mass., Acc. No. 949; 42.3 × 32.9 cm.

153. (Plate 168) *The Entombment.* Art market, Amsterdam (Goudstikker, 1930, 71 × 53.5). • Present location unknown.

154. (Plate 168) *The Entombment.* Staedelsches Kunstinstitut, Frankfurt, No. 115 (transferred from wood to canvas, 117 × 160). • Inv. No. 751.

155. (Plate 168) *The Resurrection.* O. Reinhart collection, Winterthur. • 71 × 53 cm.

156. (Plate 169) *The Last Judgment.* Municipal museum, Bruges, No. 11 (117 × 165, curved at the top). Formerly installed over the mantel of the great hall of the Bruges town hall. Judging by payment vouchers of 1524-25, Provost did this work for the jury chamber. Shown in Bruges in 1902, No. 167. See p. 86. Beneath the scene with the damned, Provost had shown a cart filled with clerics. Pieter Pourbus removed or overpainted this in 1549-50 at the behest of the municipal authorities. • Inv. No. 117; 145 × 169 cm.

b. (Plate 170) Municipal museum, Bruges, No. 16. A copy of 1578, by Jacques van de Cornehuse, for the Church of St. Donatian 1671. • Inv. No. 154; 128 × 127 cm.

157. (Plate 171) *The Last Judgment.* Institute of Arts, Detroit, No. 172 (58.5 × 61.5). From the collections of Louis Philippe of France and Niewenhuys (Brussels auction of 1883, attributed to Aeken). See p. 87. • Acc. No. 89.35.

158. (Plate 172) *The Last Judgment.* Kunsthalle, Hamburg, No. 323 (67.7 × 61). From the Abel collection, Stuttgart, and the Weber collection, Hamburg. Shown in Bruges in 1902, No. 168.

159. (Plate 172) *The Last Judgment.* Collection of Vicomte Ruffo de Bonneval, Brussels (108 × 97). Shown in Bruges in 1902, No. 169. Done at a rather early

period. Allegedly from the Dominican church in Bruges. See p. 87. • Now in a Private collection, Luxembourg.

160. (Plates 173-175) *Scenes from the Legends of St. Anthony of Padua and St. Bonaventure.* Centrepiece of an altarpiece, the shutters of which (with the donor's family) are by another later hand [68]. Brussels museum, No. 575 (191 × 140, curved at the top). Dated 1521 on the frame. The donor was Adam van Riebeke, treasurer of the city of Bruges, 1517-41, and his wife Margaret, Parmentier by birth. • Inv. No. 2588; 191 × 140—187 × 62.5 cm.

161. (Plate 176) *St. Andrew*; verso, in grisaille, *The Angel of the Annunciation*, Art market, Amsterdam (Goudstikker, 1923, 65 × 39). • Now in the Bisschoppelijk Museum, Haarlem, on loan from the Dienst voor 's Rijks Verspreide Kunstvoorwerpen, The Hague, Inv. Nos. 8785, 8784; 64.5 × 37 cm [69].

162. (Plate 177) *St. Jerome Chastising Himself*, outdoors. Auctioned at Kleykamp, The Hague, 1924, No. 22, attributed to Isenbrant. • Present location unknown.

163. (Plate 177). *St. Andrew*, with another saint, a clerical donor and the Virgin on clouds. Private ownership, Hamburg (32.5 × 27). • Now in the P. de Boer collection, Amsterdam.

164. (Plate 177) *The Virgin Enthroned.* H. H. Lehman collection, New York (97 × 65). Copied in part after Rogier van der Weyden, the landscape after the St. Luke panel. The figure presumably also goes back to Rogier and is similarly represented by the Master of the Embroidered Foliage (my Vol. IV, No. 84, plate 77). From a rather early period. The authorship is unmistakable, from the Virgin's head.
• Present location unknown.

165. (Plate 177) *Virgin and Child*, before a flowering hedge. A. Lehman collection, New York (31.5 × 17). From the Gotisches Haus, Wörlitz. Done at a rather early period. • Present location unknown.

166. (Plate 178) *Virgin and Child in a Church*, standing on an altar. Cremona museum, No. 240 (about 100 × 80). Reproduced in Dülberg, *Frühholländer in Italien*, Pl. 23.

167. (Plate 178) *Virgin and Child Enthroned*, by a fountain. Piacenza museum.
• 27 × 18 cm [70].

168. (Plate 179) *Virgin and Child, Seated Outdoors.* National Gallery, London, No. 713 (61 × 48). • 60.5 × 50 cm.

169. (Plate 180) *Virgin and Child.* National Gallery, Edinburgh, No. 1537, acquired in 1921 (34 × 20, rounded at the top). Done at a rather early period.

170. (Plate 180) *Virgin and Child*, in half-length. Strasbourg museum, No. 52 (59×42). With an Italian inscription that includes a date of 1488 suggesting that the panel was done before that year. Shown in Bruges in 1902, No. 342. Actually not done before 1500, after Rogier. See p. 90. • Inv. No. 268; 57×40 cm.

171. (Plate 180) *Virgin and Child*, in half-length, before a wall of foliage. Private ownership, West Germany. • Present location unknown.

172. (Plate 180) *Virgin and Child*, in half-length. E. Renders collection, Bruges (36×25). • Present location unknown.

173. *Virgin and Child*. Collection of Conde d'Almenas, Madrid, present whereabouts unknown. A partial copy after Jan van Eyck's van der Paele altarpiece [71].

174. (Plate 181) *Virgin and Child*, in half-length on a gilt ground. Von Pannwitz collection, De Hartekamp, near Haarlem. Formerly in the private collection of J. Böhler, Munich. In the original frame. • Now in the Hessisches Landesmuseum, Darmstadt, Inv. No. G.K. 1151; 28.4×19 cm.

175. (Plate 181) *Virgin and Child*, being crowned by two angels, fragment. Hermitage, Leningrad. • Inv. No. 405; 62×47 cm.

176. (Plate 181) *Virgin and Child*, in half-length, being crowned by angels. Kunsthalle, Karlsruhe, No. 148 (96×66). • 95×63, 1 cm (with additions), 85×57.8 cm (the original painting) [72].

177. (Plates 182, 183) *The Virgin in the Clouds*, with sibyls and prophets. Hermitage, Leningrad, No. 449 (transferred from wood to canvas, 201×159, curved at the top). From the Cathedral of St. Donatian, Bruges. Once in the collection of King William of the Netherlands, there ascribed to Quentin Massys (auction of 1850, No. 20). Probably the panel documented as having been installed in 1524 on the altar dedicated to the Prophet Daniel in St. Donatian's. See p. 87. • Inv. No. 417; 203×151 cm.

178. (Plate 184) *The Virgin Enthroned*, with St. John the Baptist, St. Jerome and the donor, a Carthusian monk. Rijksmuseum, Amsterdam, No. 1923a (75.5×65). From the C. Hoogendijk collection. About 1505. • On loan to the Koninklijk Kabinet van Schilderijen, Mauritshuis, The Hague, No. 853.

179. (Plate 185) *The Virgin and St. Joseph*, with a woman holding a child. Collection of Viscount Bearsted, London (87×31). On the verso, in grisaille, an *Annunciation*. From the collection of a nobleman in Palermo. • Upton House, National Trust, Banbury, Cat. No. 164 [73].

180. (Plate 185) *Portrait of a Man*, bust-length. Louvre, Paris No. 2204a(36×28).

On the verso, an armorial bearing and the sitter's motto. See. p. 93. • Inv. No. 1346.

181. (Plate 186) *Portrait of a Donatrix*, section from an altarpiece shutter. Baron Thyssen collection, Schloss Rohoncz (53.5 × 46). From the collection of Col. Burn Murldock, Florence. • Now in the Thyssen-Bornemisza Collection, Schloss Rohoncz Foundation, Castagnola, Cat. No. 336.

182. (Plate 186) *Portrait of a Donor*, section from an altarpiece shutter, the pendant to No. 181, above. Johnson collection, Philadelphia, Catalogue I, No. 273, ascribed to Solario (54 × 46).

183. (Plate 186) *Portrait of a Man*, bust-length. Art market, Berlin (P. Cassirer, 1929, 37.5 × 25, rounded at the top). • Now in the Heinz Kisters collection, Kreuzlingen (Switzerland).

CATALOGUE D: THE PAINTINGS OF THE SO-CALLED BRUGES MASTER OF 1500

184. (Plate 187) *The Crucifixion, Christ Carrying the Cross, The Lamentation*, on one panel. Church of the Saviour, Bruges (142 × 225). Shown in Bruges in 1902, No. 120. The original frame allegedly carried the date 1500. See p. 95.

185. (Plate 188) *Christ Shown to the People*. National Gallery, London, No. 1087 (92 × 41). In part after an engraving by Schongauer. • 93 × 41 cm.

186. (Plate 188) *The Miracle of St. Anthony and the Ass*. Prado, Madrid, No. 1917 (121 × 80).

THE PAINTINGS OF THE MASTER OF THE ANDRÉ MADONNA

187. (Plate 189) *Virgin and Child*, in half-length. Musée Jacquemart-André, Paris (43 × 31). Shown in Bruges in 1902, No. 99. See p. 96 • Inv. No. 1868 ; 44 × 32 cm.

188. (Plate 190) *The Virgin*, standing, with four angels. Baron Thyssen collection, Schloss Rohoncz (62 × 32). From the Ed. Simon collection, Berlin. • Now in the Thyssen-Bornemisza Collection, Schloss Rohoncz Foundation, Castagnola, No. 263.

189. (Plate 190) *Virgin and Child*, in half-length. R. Koeber collection, Harburg (27.5 × 17.5). • Present location unknown [74].

190. (Plate 191) *Altarpiece with Shutters, The Adoration of the Magi* : on the shutters, the donor and the donatrix with saints. Art market, Berlin (Ball, 1925, 100 × 70—30, curved at the top). • Present location unknown.

191. (Plate 192) *Altarpiece with Shutters, The Adoration of the Magi*: left shutter, *The Nativity*; right, *The Virgin*, outdoors. Collection of Baron Fürstenberg, Hugenpoet castle, Rhine Province (101 × 70—30, curved at the top).

192. (Plate 193) *Altarpiece with Shutters, Christ Shown to the People*. Prado, Madrid, No. 1559 (109 × 89—40). Free after Quentin Massys's panel in the Palace of the Doges, Venice [75].

193. (Plate 194) *Altarpiece with Shutters, The Lamentation*: on the shutters, the mourners. Chapel of St. Sang, Bruges (102 × 71—30, curved at the top). See p. 96. This is the work that has given the master his name.

a. (Plate 195) L. W. auction, Brussels, 1928, No. 65 (105 × 71—30). A fairly close replica. • Present location unknown.

b. (Plate 195) Art market, Paris (Durand Ruel, 1895, 100 × 70—30). A fairly close replica. • 100 × 71.5—32.5 cm, in 1961, New York, Art market (Durand-Ruel). Present location unknown.

In the Capilla Real in Granada is a rather crude triptych, the shutters of which coincide closely with those of the St. Sang altarpiece. • No. 8; 90.5 × 57.5—23.5 cm [76].

194. (Plate 196) *Altarpiece with Shutters, The Holy Family*, in half-length: on the shutters, Sts. Catherine and Barbara. Weber collection, Hamburg, Berlin auction, 1912, No. 74, present whereabouts unknown (105 × 75—31). Shown in Bruges in 1902, No. 260. • Now in the Kunsthalle, Hamburg, Inv. No. 7.

195. (Plates 197-199) *Altarpiece with Shutters, The Virgin Mother of God*, sibyls and prophets: left shutter, *The Emperor Augustus with the Sibyl*; right, *St. John on the Island of Patmos*; verso, *Christ Shown to the People*; *The Virgin, with Sts. John and Francis*. Bruges, St. Jacques (94.5 × 116—53). Shown in Bruges in 1902, No. 155.

196. (Plate 196) *A Pair of Altarpiece Shutters, St. Catherine, St. Barbara*. Art market, Paris (Bacri, 85 × 28 each). • Now in the Cleveland Museum of Art, Bequest of John L. Severance, Cleveland, Ohio, Acc. Nos. 42.633, 42.634; 86.3 × 29.8 cm.

197. (Plate 200) *The Adoration of the Magi*. Ambrosiana, Milan (about 100 × 140). • Inv. No. 47; 98 × 71—97 × 31 cm.

198. *The Adoration of the Magi*. Art market, London (Durlacher, 1927, 62.5 × 80). Free after Hugo van der Goes, directly or indirectly. See the panel by Gerard David in the Pinakothek, Munich. • Present location unknown.

199. (Plate 200) *Christ Shown to the People.* Art market, Paris, 1913. • Later in the Mrs. Ricardo Espírito Santo Silva collection, Lisbon, 71.1 × 55.8 cm [77].

200. (Plate 201) *Christ Carrying the Cross.* Art market, New York (Kleinberger, 1926). A wide panel (about 130 × 150, curved at the top). • Now in the Bob Jones University, Collection of Religious Paintings, Greenville, S. C., Acc. No. 55.71; 142.7 × 142.4 cm.

201. (Plate 202) *The Almighty with the Dead Saviour and Four Angels.* Brussels museum, No. 592 (93.5 × 77.5). Free after Colijn de Coter (my Vol. IV, No. 90 (Plate 84). • Inv. No. 360.

202. (Plate 202) *Christ with the Virgin and St. John.* Private ownership, Bassano (45 × 58). • Present location unknown.

203. (Plate 202) *Virgin and Child,* in half-length. P. Strauss collection, New York (48 × 33). See p. 97. • Now in the Museum of Fine Arts, Edith A. and Percy S. Straus collection, Houston, Texas, Acc. No. 44.531; 50.4 × 35.5 cm.

204. (Plate 203) *Virgin and Child,* in half-length. Art market, Berlin (Dr. Rothmann, 50 × 36). • In 1959 on the Brussels art market (A. De Heuvel Gallery). Present location unknown.

205. (Plate 203) *Virgin and Child,* knee-length. Collection of Frau Geheimrat Zimmermann, Berlin (formerly M. Jaffé). Published by Scheibler in the *Zeitschrift für Christliche Kunst,* Vol. 4, p. 137, Pl. VI, ascribed to the Master of the Death of the Virgin. • Auctioned at Parke-Bernet, New York, 28th. November 1962, No. 2; 64 × 45 cm. Present location unknown.

206. (Plate 203) *Virgin and Child,* outdoors. Private ownership, Milan (73 × 52). • Present location unknown.

207. (Plate 203) *The Holy Family,* with two angels. P. Meyerheim collection, Berlin (67 × 53). Subsequently in the Chillingworth collection, Nuremberg, present whereabouts unknown.

208. (Plate 204) *The Virgin Enthroned,* with three angels. Antwerp museum, No. 535 (79 × 55). See p. 97.

209. (Plate 204) *Virgin and Child,* with four angels. Palermo museum. • Inv. No. 68; 102.5 × 76.5 cm [78].

210. (Plate 204) *The Holy Family,* in half-length. Kunsthalle, Hamburg, No. 15 (60.5 × 46).

211. (Plate 205) *Virgin and Child with St. Bernard,* in half-length. Brussels museum, No. 547 (43 × 52). • Inv. No. 370.

212. (Plate 205) *St. Luke Painting the Virgin.* Fogg museum, Cambridge, U.S.A. (43 × 33). • Now in the Busch-Reisinger Museum, Harvard University, Purchase

Associate Fund, from Fogg Art Museum, Cambridge, Mass., Acc. No. 1965.20; 43.3 × 32.3 cm.

213. (Plate 205) *Virgin and Child with St. Anne,* Joseph, Joachim and angels. Staedelsches Kunstinstitut, Frankfurt, No. 82 (89 × 82). Once wrongly attributed to the Master of Frankfurt. • Inv. No. 970.

214. (Plate 206) *Lucretia,* in half-length. Muller de Ketelboeters auction, Brussels, 1926, No. 30 (72.5 × 57). Formerly in the van Gameren collection, Antwerp. Much in the style of Quentin Massys, possibly a copy after Massys. • Sold at the Palais des Beaux-Arts, Brussels, 11th-12th October 1955, No. 161. Present location unknown.

a. (Plate 206) Private ownership, Paris. A faithful replica, more in the master's wonted style, with the inscription: *Lucrezia—Romana—.* • Present location unknown.

215. (Plate 206) *Lucretia,* in half-length. Vienna Academy. With an inscription: *Lucrecia—Romana—.* • Inv. No. 1247; 71 × 55 cm.

216. (Plate 207) *Lucretia,* in half-length. Budapest museum, No. 692 (65 × 48.5). • Inv. No. 127.

217. *Lucretia,* in half-length.

a. (Plate 207) Collection of Professor Matsch, Vienna. • Present location unknown.

b. (Plate 207) Schleissheim (67 × 51). Dated 1523. Published by Feuchtmayr, who attributed it to the Master of the University Altarpiece, in *Beiträge zur Geschichte der Deutschen Kunst,* Vol. II, 1928, p. 20. • Now in the Bayerische Staatsgemäldesammlungen Alte Pinakothek, Munich, Inv. No. 1431 [79].

c. J. J. Lichtmann auction, Vienna, 1917, No. 37. • Present location unknown [80].

d. Bolten collection, London. • Present location unknown [81].

These replicas coincide precisely. The left hand is exactly as in the works listed as Nos. 214 and 215, which otherwise differ in composition.

CATALOGUE E: THE PAINTINGS OF JOACHIM PATENIER

218. (Plates 208-210) *Altarpiece with Shutters, Virgin and Child,* on the flight into Egypt: left shutter, *St. John the Baptist*; right, *Pope Cornelius.* Von Kaufmann collection, Berlin, damaged by fire in 1904 (110 × 72—30). Shown in Bruges in 1902,

No. 199. • Now in the W. Kaus collection, Frankfurt.

a. (Plate 208) Art market, Amsterdam (Goudstikker, 1928, 31 × 20—9, rounded at the top). An altarpiece, the centrepiece of which is a free copy of the one in the von Kaufmann triptych [82]. • Later in the A. Kleiweg de Zwaan collection, Doorn, Netherlands. Present location unknown.

219. (Plate 211) *Landscape with Sodom on Fire.* Koenigs collection, Haarlem (23 × 29.5). • On loan from the Dienst voor 's Rijks Verspreide Kunstvoorwerpen, The Hague to the Museum Boymans-van Beuningen, Rotterdam, Inv. No. 2312.

220. (Plate 212) *St. John the Baptist Preaching.* R. L. Taylor collection, Philadelphia (38 × 50.5). At lower right the same arms as in the picture in the Johnson Collection, No. 226, below, perhaps appertaining to a proprietor of the two panels (Lucas Rem ?). • Now in the Museum of Art, Philadelphia, Pa., Acc. No. 44—9—2.

a. (Plate 213) Art market, Munich (J. Böhler, 1915, 38 × 45). A replica of equal merit, slightly cropped on both sides. From the Peltzer collection. • Now in the Musées Royaux des Beaux-Arts de Belgique, Brussels, Inv. No. 6178; 35.3 × 45.2 cm.

b. (Plate 213) Art market, Munich (J. Böhler, 1917, 20 × 30). A fairly close replica. • Present location unknown.

221. (Plate 216) *The Baptism of Christ.* Staatliche Galerie, Vienna, No. 666 (68 × 77). Signed: OPUS · JOACHIM · D · PATINIER. See p. 101. • Inv. No. 981 in the Gemäldegalerie im Kunsthistorischen Museum, 59.5 × 77 cm [83].

222. (Plate 214) *Landscape with St. John the Baptist Preaching.* Uppsala, University. Judged only from a photograph. Possibly an original [84]. • Inv. No. L 270/71; 31 × 35 cm.

223. (Plate 215) *Landscape with the Baptism of Christ.* Uppsala, University. Judged only from a photograph. Apparently an original [85]. • Inv. No. L 270/71; 31 × 35 cm.

224. (Plate 217) *The Crucifixion*, with the executioners and mourners. Schlayer collection, Madrid (71 × 59, top corners chamfered). • Now in the Portland Art Museum, Portland, Oregon, Acc. No. 41.7.

225. (Plate 217) *Christ Carrying the Cross.* Von Schwabach collection, Berlin. From the Schacky collection, auction of 1914, No. 67. • Present location unknown, 21 × 37 cm.

a. Art market, London (Arnot, 1928, 24.5 × 37). A fairly close replica. • Present location unknown.

226. (Plate 218) *Assumption of the Virgin*, with apostles. In small tondos, upper left, *The Nativity*, right, *The Resurrection.* Johnson collection, Philadelphia, Cata-

logue II, No. 378 (57 × 55). From the C. T. Yerkes collection, 1909. Lower right, arms displaying a bull (see No. 220, above). Valentiner, in the Johnson Catalogue, gives the figures to another hand, that of an Antwerp Mannerist.

227. (Plate 219) *Virgin and Child*, in half-length. Art market, Amsterdam (Goudstikker, 1920, 34 × 24.5). From the Heseltine collection, London. Shown at Bruges in 1902, No. 211. • Present location unknown.

a. (Plate 219) Collection of Countess Sierstorpff, Eltville. The figure in a different style, the landscape in the manner of Patenier. • Present location unknown.

228. (Plate 219) *The Flight into Egypt*, the Holy Family at rest. Institute of Arts, Minneapolis (35 × 50). The landscape with the figures in the background is exactly as in the centrepiece of the Kaufmann altarpiece. The Virgin differs and is manifestly by another hand. • Acc. No. 14.2 in the Minneapolis Institute of Arts, The William Hood Dunwoody Fund, Minneapolis, Minnesota, 34.2 × 48.8 cm.

229. *The Holy Family in a Landscape*. Art market, Munich (Böhler, 36 × 44). • In 1922 in the W. van der Linden collection, Rotterdam. Present location unknown.

230. *Rest on the Flight into Egypt*. Berlin art market (Blumenreich, 33 × 20). The figure group after Schongauer's engraving B. 7. • Present location unknown.

231. (Plate 220) *The Flight into Egypt*. Antwerp museum, No. 64 (17 × 21). Inscribed: *Opus·Joachim·D·Patinir.*

232. (Plate 221) *Virgin and Child*, resting on the flight. Baron Thyssen collection, Schloss Rohoncz (30 × 56). From the von Kaufmann and Ed. Simon collections, Berlin. Shown in Bruges in 1902, No. 200. • No. 321 in the Thyssen-Bornemisza Collection, Schloss Rohoncz Foundation, Castagnola, 31.5 × 57.5 cm [86].

233. (Plate 222) *Virgin and Child*, resting on the flight. Art market, Berlin (Dr. Bloch, 1929, 21.5 × 38). The figure by another hand, in the style of Joos van Cleve, like the Madonna in the Brussels picture, No. 49, above. • Now in the Museum Ridder Smidt van Gelder, Antwerp, Inv. No. SM/960.

234. (Plate 223) *Virgin and Child*, resting on the flight. Johnson collection, Philadelphia, Catalogue II, No. 377 (44 × 57). • 46.3 × 60.6 cm.

235. (Plates 224, 225) *Virgin and Child*, resting on the flight. Prado, Madrid, No. 1611 (121 × 177). See p. 106.

236. *Virgin and Child*, resting on the flight. Art market, Berlin (Blumenreich, 1930, 128 × 113.5). The figure of the Virgin apparently inserted by another hand. • Present location unknown [87].

237. (Plates 226, 227) *Virgin and Child*, resting on the flight. Gemäldegalerie, Berlin, No. 608 (62 × 78). The basket on the ground exactly as in the Kaufmann altarpiece and in the Holy Family panel in the Prado. • Now in the Gemäldegalerie der Staatlichen Museen, Berlin-Dahlem.

238. (Plate 228) *Virgin and Child*, resting on the flight. Fr. Steinmeyer collection, Lucerne. The Virgin in the style of Joos van Cleve. • Now in the Nationalmuseum, Stockholm, No. 3333; 21.5 × 31 cm.

239. (Plate 228) *St. Jerome*, outdoors. Karlsruhe museum, No. 144 (13 × 17). Inscribed: *opus Joachim D. Patinir*. Described by Baldass as a youthful work.

240. (Plates 230, 231) *St. Jerome*, outdoors. Prado, Madrid, No. 1614 (74 × 91). From the Escorial. See p. 104 [88].

241. (Plate 229) *St. Jerome*, outdoors. Art market, Berlin (P. Cassirer, 1926). Possibly in a fragmentary state. • In 1963 on the New York art market (Wildenstein), 34.9 × 27.3 cm. Present location unknown.

a. (Plate 229) Giroux auction, Brussels, 3rd-5th May 1927, No. 334 (41 × 50). A replica with differences, considerably wider on both sides. • Chambéry-Geneva, Mr. and Mrs. T. Kreuger collection.

242. (Plate 234) *St. Jerome*, outdoors. v. Kühlmann collection, Berlin. • Present location unknown.

243. (Plate 232) *St. Jerome in a Landscape*. Elberfeld museum (21 × 31). In 1916 on the Munich art market. • Now in the Von der Heydt-Museum der Stadt Wuppertal, Wuppertal-Elberfeld, Inv. No. G 369; 21.5 × 32 cm.

a. (Plate 233) H. Oppenheimer collection, London. A replica of the left side only, of equal merit. • Now in the National Gallery, London, No. 4826; 36.5 × 34 cm [89].

b. (Plate 232) Duensing collection, Boizenburg (25 × 34). A replica of equal merit, with minor differences. An *Assumption of the Egyptian Mary* forms a pendant (251, Plate 232) • Now in the Ruzicka-Stiftung, Kunsthaus, Zürich, Inv. No. R. 23 [90].

244. (Plate 234) *St. Jerome in a Landscape*. Private collection, Rome. Known to me only from the reproduction in Hoogewerff, Onze Kunst, Vol. XLIII, 1926, Fig. 9. • Now in the Nelson Gallery-Atkins Museum, Nelson Fund, Kansas City, Mo., Acc. No. 61-1; 35 × 49 cm.

245. (Plate 238) *St. Jerome in a Landscape*. Louvre, Paris. A recent acquisition, gift of Sir Joseph Duveen. • Inv. No. R. F. 2.429; 76 × 137 cm.

a. (Plate 238) Cà d'Oro, Venice. A smaller replica with minor differences. • No. 134 in the Giorgio Franchetti Galleria alla Cà d'Oro, 29 × 55 cm.

246. (Plates 235-237) *St. Christopher.* Escorial (about 100 × 150). See p. 105. ● 127 × 172 cm.

247. (Plate 239) *St. Christopher.* Art market, Berlin (Haberstock, 1929, 36 × 46). From private hands in Vienna. ● Present location unknown [91].

248. (Plate 239) *St. Christopher.* Chiaramonte Bordonaro collection, Palermo. Reproduced in Dülberg, *Frühholländer in Italien*, Pl. 18. My judgment of this work is based solely on the poor reproduction. It seems to be close to the St. Christopher in the Escorial. ● 46 × 56 cm.

249. (Plate 239) *Two Hermits in a Landscape.* Art market, Berlin (Blumenreich. 1929, 29 × 38). ● Present location unknown.

250. (Plate 240) *The Martyrdom of St. Catherine.* Staatliche Galerie, Vienna, No. 665 (28 × 49). ● Inv. No. 1002 in the Gemäldegalerie im Kunsthistorischen Museum, 26.8 × 44 cm [92].

a. (Plate 240) Art market, London (Douglas). A faithful replica of equal merit. ● Now in the S. Simon collection, Belgium, 37.7 × 48.8 cm.

251. (Plate 232) *Assumption of the Egyptian Mary.* Duensing collection, Boizenburg (36 × 25.5). Pendant to No. 243b, above. ● Now in the Ruzicka-Stiftung, Kunsthaus, Zurich, Inv. No. R. 24, 25.8 × 36 cm.

252. (Plate 241) *Assumption of the Egyptian Mary.* Crespi collection, Milan, present whereabouts unknown. Inscribed *Savery* in an incompatible style. A restorer may have changed *Patenier* to *Savery*. ● 31 × 70 cm.

253. (Plate 242) *River Styx.* Prado, Madrid, No. 1616 (64 × 103). From the Palace, Madrid. See p. 102.

254. (Plate 241) *Tobias and the Angel in a Landscape.* Oeffentliche Kunstsammlung, Basle (Bachofen-Burckhardt bequest, 33 × 46.5). The landscape may be by Patinier himself, the figures are by another hand. ● Inv. No. 1251.

255. (Plate 243) *Stormy Seascape with Rocky Shores*, a whale and a sailing-ship. Von Hevesy collection, Paris (30 × 21). ● Now in the S. Simon collection Belgium, 22.5 × 32.5 cm.

256. (Plate 243) *Landscape with Hunting Scenes.* Wesendonk collection, Berlin (44 × 55). ● Now in the Mr. and Mrs. C. K. Wilmers collection, Geneva.

257. (Plate 244) *Landscape with Genrelike Figures.* Art market, Amsterdam (de Boer, 1931, 29 × 42). The figures (about 1520) exactly as in the picture in the Wesendonk collection, No. 256, above. ● Present location unknown.

SUPPLEMENT TO THE CATALOGUES

JAN JOEST

Supp. 258. (Plate 246) *Altarpiece with Shutters, The Nativity.* Pinakothek, Munich. • Inv. No. 1415 in the Bayerische Staatsgemäldesammlungen, Alte Pinakothek, 46.2 × 27.5—46 × 13 cm.

JOOS VAN CLEVE

Apart from copies, Joos van Cleve's very voluminous œuvre may now be expanded by several fine portraits:

Supp. 259. (Plate 248) *Portrait of a Gentleman Removing a Ring.* Art market, London, 1934 (Asscher & Welker). About 1512. • Present location unknown.

Supp. 260. (Plate 247) *Portrait of a Gentleman Putting on a Glove.* Lugano, Schloss Rohoncz Collection (Baron Thyssen) (60 × 44). About 1515. • Now in the Kunstmuseum, Düsseldorf, Bentinck-Thyssen collection.

Supp. 261. (Plate 248) *Portrait of a Lady Holding a Rosary and a Plant.* Art market, London 1933 (Duits—38 × 28). About 1515. • Present location unknown.

JAN PROVOST

Supp. 262. (Plate 148) *Birth of the Virgin.* Art market, London, 1936 (Bloch—33 × 19). Rather early. • Later in the Museum Boymans-van Beuningen, Rotterdam, Inv. No. 2479 [93]; stolen in 1960.

Supp. 263. *Adoration of the Magi.* Baldwin collection, New Orleans. • Now in the Mr. and Mrs. Robert B. Baldwin collection, Slidell, Louisiana.

Supp. 264. (Plate 249) *The Lamentation.* Palermo Museum. • Inv. No. 69; 66 × 51.5 cm [94].

Supp. 265. (Plate 249) *Angel of the Annunciation.* Art market, Amsterdam, 1937 (de Boer). In grisaille (74 × 28). • Present location unknown.

JOACHIM PATENIER [95]

Supp. 266. (Plates 250, 251) *Altarpiece with Shutters, St. Jerome Chastising Himself,* outdoors: left, *The Baptism of Christ*; right, *St. Anthony.* Metropolitan Museum, New York, acquired in 1936. An important work by this master, which had drawn little attention at the collegiate church at Kremsmünster. The figures are also by him. On the versos of the shutters, in grisaille, *Virgin and Child with St. Anne*, and a holy pilgrim with a model of a church (St. Sebaldus?). • No. 36.14

A-C in the Metropolitan Museum of Art, Fletcher Fund, 120.3 × 81.2—121.9 × 36.8 cm.

Two replicas of the *Landscape with Sodom on Fire* (No. 219), both in tondo frames, have turned up, one (Supp. 267, Plate 211) on the art market in Cologne in 1935 (Malmedé), the other (Supp. 268, Plate 211) in Berlin in 1932 (de Burlet)—it was exhibited in Zurich in 1934. • Supp. 267 now in the Ashmolean Museum of Art, Department of Western Art, Oxfort, No. 320; diam, 34 cm. Supp. 268 now in the Dr. H. C. Walter Boveri collection, Zurich, 56.5 × 70 cm.
One of these paintings may be the one Dürer received as a gift in Antwerp, *das klein gemalt Täfelein, das Meister Joachim gemacht hat, ists Loth mit den Töchtern.*

Supp. 269. (Plate 252), Supp. 270. Two wide paintings, landscape pendants, were recently sold in Venice (36 × 100 each). • One of these landscapes was auctioned at Sotheby's, London, on 4th July 1956, No. 39. Present location unknown.

ADDENDA

o Add. 271. (Plate 252) *The Nativity*, drawing, Leningrad, The Hermitage, Inv. No. 7528; 695 × 530 mm. Jan Joest. Cf. Max J. Friedländer, 'Eine Zeichnung von Jan Joest von Kalkar', in *Oud-Holland*, LVII, 1940, pp. 160-167.

• Add. 272. (Plate 253) *The Flight into Egypt*. Ponce, Puerto Rico, Museo de Arte, The Luis A. Ferre Foundation, Inc., Inv. No. 58.0045; 64.8 × 44.5 cm. Joos van Cleve. Cf. J. S. Held, 'A New Museum in Ponce', in *The Burlington Magazine*, CIII, 1961, p. 317.

• Add. 273 A. (Plate 149) *The Presentation in the Temple*. Laren, Prof. H. J. Hellema collection, 34 × 19 cm. Jan Provost. Cf. *Museum Boymans-van Beuningen Rotterdam, Catalogus Schilderijen tot 1800*, Rotterdam, 1962, p. 106.

• Add. 273 B. *Adoration of the Magi* and *Tobit with the Angel*. London, auction Leonard Gow at Christie's 28th May 1937, 25.5 × 28.5 cm. Present location unknown. Jan Provost. Cf. G. Ring, 'Additions to the Work of Jan Provost and Quentin Massys. I. Jan Provost: A Series of Panels from His Early Period', in *The Burlington Magazine*, XXIX 1941, pp. 156-160 [196].

• Add. 274. (Plate 176) *St. Christopher. Verso, a Virgin from an Annunciation.* Madrid, Museo del Prado, Pablo Bosch Bequest, No. 67, Inv. No. 2699; 62 × 36 cm, pendant to No. 161. Jan Provost. Cf. S. J. Gudlaugson, 'Het bij Friedländer, Jan Provost Nr. 161 behorende altaarstuk. Mededelingen van het Rijksbureau voor Kunsthistorische Documentatie', in *Oud-Holland*, XXII, 1957, pp. 239, 2440.

Editor's Note

JAN JOEST

In attributing a drawing [97] to Jan Joest, Friedländer himself [98] took occasion to define more precisely the links between this painter and Derick Baegert on one hand, and between Barthel Bruyn and Joos van Cleve on the other. Probably a native of Wesel, Jan Joest without a doubt studied with Baegert, apparently a close kinsman. Joest himself was the teacher of Barthel Bruyn, probably his son-in-law, and took Joos van Cleve into his workshop as a journeyman.

Similar problems concerning the origins and influence of Jan Joest were discussed at about the same time in a monograph by C. P. Baudisch [99]. Here the painter's whole œuvre is thoroughly analyzed, in particular the two most important works, the altarpieces at Calcar and Palencia. Baudisch included transcriptions of many documents relating to Jan Joest.

The unique position of Jan Joest accounts for his inclusion in two books of a more general character, the first by G. J. Hoogewerff [100], concerning painting in the North Netherlands, the second by A. Stange [101], devoted to German painting. Hoogewerff suggests in his study that the youthful Jan Joest may have been the Master of St. John the Evangelist, who was active in Genoa at the end of the 15th century [102]. This suggestion seems to have found little acceptance [103]. As for Stange, he insists that Jan Joest belongs to the school of the Lower Rhine—at least by origin and training. Stange enlarges the master's œuvre by the attribution of several religious paintings [104] and more particularly some portraits [105], showing Joest in a hitherto unfamiliar light. In a later publication [106], Stange reverts to the question of portraits that may have been done by Jan Joest [107].

Documents are, of course, sometimes subject to divergent interpretations, since the names of some of the painters mentioned may be ambiguous. Thus J. Bruyn [108] expresses some doubt that Jan Joest lived in Haarlem from 1509 onwards, as a painter of that name mentioned in a Haarlem document probably was a mere namesake.

Restoration work on the Calcar altarpiece (No. 1) in 1961/63 has been followed by the publication of a detailed account providing full technical information [109].

Studying the Palencia altarpiece (No. 2), Ramon Revilla Vielva [110] sees the hand of another painter in the portrait of the donor, possibly Juan de Flandes.

We must mention lastly, that Chandler R. Post [111] gives to Jan Joest four panels of an altarpiece showing *The Legend of St. Bartholemew*, in the church of San Lesmes in Burgos, and that P. Quarré [112] ascribes to the same painter a *Taking of Christ* [113].

A few authors [114] have expressed doubt about the identification of the Master of the Death of the Virgin as Joos van Cleve; but H. Gerson [115] cites a new argument in its favour. Actually, even Constantyn Huygens, in a letter of 15th April 1653 mentions the attribution to Joos van Cleve of two portraits, now in the National Gallery of Art, Washington (No. 117), that are generally accepted as works by the Master of the Death of the Virgin. J. Białostocki [115a] puts a new argument forward in favour of Joos van Cleve's presence in the workshop of Jan Joest of Calcar before 1509. The same author points out the existence of the portrait of Joos van Cleve on the panel showing *The Raising of Lazarus* from the Calcar altarpiece. Moreover certain figures of *The Descent of the Holy Spirit* on the versos of this panel show a striking analogy with some of the Reinhold altarpiece by Joos van Cleve (No. 20).

Joos van Cleve was inscribed as a master in Antwerp in 1511; and W. R. Valentiner [116] suggests that the *Joos van Wezele* registered the previous year as an apprentice of Simon van Herlam may have been none other than Joos van Cleve himself. Valentiner proposes that Simon van Herlam was the Master of the Morrison Triptych, and such a master-and-disciple relation would help to explain certain elements in the work of Joos van Cleve that appear to have been taken over from the Master of the Morrison Triptych.

There is no unimpeachable documentary evidence that Joos van Cleve went to Italy. G. J. Hoogewerff [117] suggested that there was a trip about 1512-1515, but has revised his opinion in a later publication [118]. He now thinks that the pictures Joos was commissioned to paint by Italian patrons are to be divided into two groups: those painted about 1515 and those dating from about 1525-1528. This implies two rather long stays in the Italian peninsula.

G. Marlier [119] has studied the Italian influence upon Joos van Cleve, and in particular that of Leonardo. He believes that Joos's visit to Fontainebleau (±1531-1535) may be sufficent to explain these influences; but he adds that the Italian elements are so numerous that a journey to Italy—before Fontainebleau—seems more likely. E. P. Richardson [120] suggests that Joos van Cleve stopped off in England on his way back from Fontainebleau to the Netherlands.

The self-portraits which Joos inserted in quite a few of his paintings give a clue for a chronology of the artist's œuvre. J. Białostocki [121] thinks that the portrait of St. Reinhold in the Gdansk altarpiece (No. 20) is a portrait of the painter. He also suggests that the altarpiece which bears a monogram was put there by the end of 1516. Białostocki also discusses the various influences to which Joos van Cleve was exposed and dwells on the fact that the influence of Leonardo was already evident about 1515, some time before his journey to Italy. On the other hand, Joos van Cleve seems not to have been in contact with Patenier prior to 1515, as some authors wish to believe [122]. J. Snyder [123] insists on the important rôle played by Joos van Cleve in the development of landscape.

I. Bergström [124] and C. G. Stridbeck [125] have thrown light on the symbolic meanings of certain objects in some of Joos van Cleve's compositions. J. Hand [126] presents a thorough iconological analysis of a *St. Jerome* (No. 40) and places this religious scene within the historical context of its time.

Some of Joos's portraits have been identified: H. Gerson [127] has discovered that the names of the sitters for the two portraits formerly in the Liechtenstein Gallery (No. 117) are Joris W. Vezeler and Margaretha Boghe; and J. Rosenberg [128] sees in the *Portrait of a Man* from the Winthrop collection (No. 74) the likeness of Roger Count of Blitterswijk-Gelderen [129]. S. Bergmans identifies the sitter of the *Portrait of a Man* (No. 93) as Sir Thomas Wyat the Younger [129a].

A. Staring [130] shows that two portraits given to Joos van Cleve, those of Eleonore of France [131], wife of Francis I (No. 108) and of Mencia Mendoça, wife of Henry II of Nassau (No. 109), reach back to Jan Gossart rather than only to the painter himself. This implies that Joos may have copied the portrait of Eleonore before going to Fontainebleau. The original portrait of Mencia Mendoça, by Gossart, seems to have been conceived as a pendant to a portrait of Henry II of Nassau [132].

Joos van Cleve is the recipient of numerous attributions. Keeping to the rules of this edition, we limit ourselves to only those that have already been published [133]: a triptych with a *Holy Family* [134], a *Last Judgment* [135], a *Boy Jesus with Grapes* [136], a *Jesus and John as Boys, Kissing* [137], a *St. Jerome* [138], another *St. Jerome* [139], a *Portrait of a Nude Lady*, in half-length [140] and two *Portraits of Francis I* [141].

CORNELIS VAN CLEVE

A first attempt to list a number of works under the name of Cornelis van Cleve was made by Friedländer in volume XIV [141a]. Some years later, he devoted an article to the painter, in an effort to define his character and development more closely [142]. Cornelis van Cleve owed much to his father, in whose workshop he was trained and in time turned more and more towards Italian art, in particular Andrea del Sarto, on whose composition he drew more than once [143].

Some other authors have also shown interest in Cornelis van Cleve and attributed paintings to him: a *Dance of Children* [144], a *Virgin and Child* [145], a *Holy Family* [146], and a series of *Portraits of Sir Thomas Wyat* [147].

JAN PROVOST

Our knowledge of Jan Provost's life has been enriched by publication of a series of documents discovered in the municipal archives of Bruges [148].

The beginnings and development of Jan Provost and the influences he underwent have stirred the interest of a number of art historians. F. Bologna [149] finds some relation between the work of the young Provost and Simon Marmion and stresses the links that must have existed between Provost and some of the leading artists of the Antwerp and Bruges schools, in particular Quentin Massys, Joos van Cleve, Joachim Patenier and Gerard David [150]. S. Speth-Holterhoff [151] also recognizes the influence of Simon Marmion. Jan Provost may have met his senior in the workshop of Pilavaine, publisher of manuscripts in Mons, where Simon Marmion seems to have worked.

Some works of Jan Provost have been dismembered. C. L. Ragghianti [152] and G. J. Hoogewerff [153] offer a partial reconstruction of a large triptych originally from the church of St. Colombano in Genoa and composed of a central panel

showing an *Annunciation* (No. 140) and two wings, of which only fragments are preserved, namely a *St. Peter* (No. 137) and a *Donor* (No. 182) from the left shutter, and a *St. Elizabeth* (No. 137) and a *Donatrix* (No. 181) from the right one. The versos of these wings showed two saints, in grisaille.

Two panels, at the Louvre and the Prado (No. 129) are fragments from the wings of a polyptych of the *Holy Kindred* which belonged to the collections of Philip II at the Madrid Alcazar [154]. Thanks to a description found by F. J. Sanchez Cantón in an inventory of the possessions of this king, it has been possible to identify the figures. The Zacharias and St. Bernardin of Siena on the Madrid panel and Emerence and St. Clare on the one in Paris. P. Pieper [155] suggests that a fragment [156] acquired by the Landesmuseum in Münster, representing St. Anne, may come from the same polyptych [157].

Friedländer gave a single number (No. 127) to three small panels now dispersed. G. Ring [158] adds to this ensemble a panel published by Friedländer in his volume XIV (Supp. 262), and another showing two subjects, *The Adoration of the Magi* and *Tobit and the Angel* (Add. 273B) [159], while the catalogue of the Boymans-van Beuningen Museum in Rotterdam [160] mentions a sixth panel, a *Presentation in the Temple* (Add. 273A).

Basing herself on radiographs, N. Verhaegen [161] has been able to establish that a *St. John the Baptist* and a *St. Margaret of Antioch* are hidden behind a layer of paint on the versos of the wings of the triptych with the *Adoration of the Magi* (No. 124).

A study of the restoration of the *Last Judgment* at the Bruges Museum (No. 156) by A. Janssens de Bisthoven [162] reports in particular on the cleaning of the *Hell*, in the right corner of the panel, which was overpainted by Pieter Pourbus in 1550.

J. Marrow [163] calls attention to a panel by Jan Provost in the Enschede Museum (No. 136) in which St. John the Baptist carries a lantern. Although this attribute also appears in some other examples, it is rather uncommon.

Apart from the attributions already mentioned and those included in the Addenda, we wish to add a *Virgin and Child with an Angel, St. John the Baptist and a Donor* [164]; a *Virgin and Child* [165]; another *Virgin and Child* [166]; a triptych with a *Virgin Enthroned with St. John the Baptist and St. John the Evangelist* and on the versos an *Annunciation* [167]; a *Nativity* [168]; a *Lamentation* [169]; a *Last Judgment* and a *Virgin as the Patroness of the Cistercian Order* [170].

THREE BRUGES MASTERS

These three masters were well represented in the exhibition *Anonieme Vlaamse Primitieven* organized in Bruges in 1969. The catalogue [171], published in both

Dutch and French, discusses them in the light of the latest knowledge and the works shown are fully analyzed.

The œuvre of the Master of 1500, now renamed more fittingly the Master of the Scenes of the Bruges Passion [172], is very limited. C. L. Ragghianti [173] has attempted to enlarge it by including with it the paintings by the Master of the Turin Adoration [174].

The many well-known borrowings which characterize the compositions of this painter are copiously illustrated in an article by H. Demoriane [175].

The Christ shown to the People (No. 185) is discussed in detail in the *Corpus de la Peinture des Anciens Pays-Bas Méridionaux au Quinzième Siècle* devoted to the London National Gallery [176].

Little is to be said about the Master of the André Madonna. The Christ child shown writing in the painting at the Musée Jacquemart-André in Paris, is listed in a study by Parkhurst [177] as a rather archaic example of this master's iconography. The composition of the *Virgin Standing*, in the Thyssen collection (No. 188), is derived from a prototype attributed to Gerard David [178].

The theme of Lucretia stubbing herself, very popular since the 16th century [179], and the motive of the convex mirror [180] have been the object of iconographical studies in which some compositions of the Master of St. Sang are mentioned as examples.

JOACHIM PATENIER

None could have supplemented Friedländer's text on Patenier better than Friedländer himself. Readers should refer to his *Essays* in which he touches upon the various genres, most importantly landscape [181].

The only monograph on Patenier published since 1937, surprisingly, is one by R. A. Koch [182]. Approaching his subject from various angles—the biographical data, the painter's formative years [182a], the datings of his works and their chronology, his workshop, his collaboration with other painters, etc.—the author arrives at an image of the painter somewhat different from that sketched by Friedländer. He also eliminates a number of works from Patenier's œuvre, giving some to the Master of the Female Half-Lengths, who is thus seen in a new light, especially as a landscape painter [183].

In the meantime the painter has been the subject of some less thorough articles and studies by A. Piron [184], Ed. Gérard [185], A. Barret [186] and M. Kunel [187].

The rôle played by Patenier in the evolution of landscape painting could scarcely escape the attention of specialists and has, in fact, intrigued some of them: C. van de Wetering [188], G. J. Hoogewerff [189], G. Künstler [190], H. Franz [191], F. M. Godfrey [192].

The two paintings at Uppsala University (Nos. 222 and 223) originally forming a single panel, have been reassembled again, on the occasion of a restoration in 1953. Friedländer's tentative attribution, it will be recalled, was made without first-hand knowledge of the works. According to Å. Bengtsson [193], following this restoration, there can be no doubt that these paintings are indeed originals [194]. For some details in the landscape of the *St. Jerome* in the Prado (No. 240), Patenier seems to have drawn his inspiration from actual scenery near Namur [195]. On the other hand, La Sainte-Baume, in Provence, according to the legend a place where the Magdalene lived, appears in two of Patenier's compositions, only one of which refers to the legend [196], *The Ecstasy of Mary Magdalene* (No. 251) [197] and *Virgin and Child Resting on the Flight* (No. 237) [198]. Patenier's knowledge of the site may derive from some other drawing by a painter, by a personal visit to Provence or by Patenier passing that way on his return from Italy. The possibility of a stay in Italy was envisaged by G. J. Hoogewerff [199], but opinions on this matter differ. R. A. Koch [200] and Å. Bengtsson [201] favour the possibility of such a stay.

Let us mention, lastly, the few attributions that have been the subjects of publications: *Virgin and Child Resting on the Flight* (Leningrad, The Hermitage, Inv. No. 3085; 51 × 96 cm) [202]; another *Virgin and Child Resting on the Flight* (Rio de Janeiro, Museu Nacional de Belas Artes, Inv. No. 3.587; 64.5 × 49.5 cm) [203]; *The Judgment of Paris* (Toledo, The Toledo Museum of Art, 32 × 43 cm) [204].

Notes

1. The present edition has adopted the principle of reproducing, in so far as possible, the totality of the paintings listed by Friedländer.

2. The predella of the Calcar altarpiece originally carried shutters also painted by Jan Joest. When the altarpiece was restored in 1676, these disappeared. A second restoration was undertaken by Stanislas de Pereira. See H. P. Hilger, *Die Denkmäler des Rheinlandes, Kreis Kleve 2*, 1964, pp. 19-21.

3. Concerning the attributions made by the Boisserées, see S. Sulzberger, 'La Réhabilitation des Primitifs Flamands, 1802-1867', (*Académie Royale de Belgique, Classe des Beaux-Arts. Mémoires*, XII), Brussels, 1961, pp. 72-74.

4. J. Białostocki too suggests that it may be a workshop product. See J. Białostocki, 'New Observations on Joos van Cleve', in *Mededelingen van het Rijksbureau voor Kunsthistorische Documentatie, Oud-Holland*, LXX, 1955, p. 121, and idem, 'Une Oeuvre de Joos van Cleve dans l'église Notre-Dame de Gdansk', in *Studia Pomorskie*, Vol. I, Wroclaw-Cracow, 1959, pp. 226-228.

5. Sir Martin Davies considers Friedländer's arguments not fully convincing. See Martin Davies, *National Gallery Catalogues. Early Netherlandish School*, 3rd ed., London, 1968, p. 69.

6. J. Białostocki does not accept the chronology suggested by Baldass and Friedländer and based on an analysis of the self-portraits. See J. Białostocki, 'New Observations on Joos van Cleve', in *Mededelingen van het Rijksbureau voor Kunsthistorische Documentatie, Oud-Holland*, LXX, 1955, pp. 121-125, and idem, 'Une Oeuvre de Joos van Cleve dans l'église Notre-Dame de Gdansk', in *Studia Pomorskie*, Vol. I, Wroclaw-Cracow, 1959, pp. 226-228.

7. It is known that Quentin Massys also painted a *St. Jerome*, but the picture is lost. See *Le Journal de Voyage 1520-1521 d'Albert Dürer dans les Anciens Pays-Bas*, translated and annotated by J.-A. Goris and G. Marlier, Brussels, 1970, pp. 21-23.

8. G. J. Hoogewerff considers the landscape very close to Patenier. In fact, the ivy-covered tree and the spring in the foreground recur in Patenier's *Flight into Egypt*, in the Prado. See G. J. Hoogewerff, '*Het Landschap van Bosch tot Rubens*', Antwerp, 1954, pp. 26 and 27.

9. S. Bergmans suggests a date of 1542 or 1548 for this portrait and identifies the sitter as Sir Thomas Wyat, portrayed by *Sotte Cleef*. See S. Bergmans, 'De Quelques Portraits Inconnus de Sir Thomas Wyat le Jeune et de Leur Attribution', in *Apollo*, Brussels, September 1941, No. 4, pp. 8-11.

10. On this subject see C. P. Baudisch, *Jan Joest von Kalkar*, Bonn, 1940, pp. 122-131.

11. According to Stange, Jan Joest must be considered as a master from the Lower Rhine. See A. Stange, *Deutsche Malerei der Gotik*, Vol. 6, Munich-Berlin, 1954, pp. 63-72.

12. G. Marlier places the picture '...in the great international movement of Mannerism, which also embraces the first Fontainebleau School'. See G. Marlier, 'Joos van Cleve—Fontainebleau and Italy', in *The Connoisseur*, Vol. 165, No. 663, May 1967, pp. 24-27.

13. Present location unknown.

14. Present location unknown, 43 × 32 cm.

15. No. 1504; 43 × 32,5 cm.

16. For the paintings given to this follower of Joos van Cleve, see the catalogue of Cornelis van Cleve, pp. 72-74.

17. No. 768 in the Kunsthistorisches Museum.

18. Perhaps to be read 'Massys' instead 'Leonardo'.

19. See note 17.

20. See C. P. Baudisch, *Jan Joest von Kalkar*, Bonn 1940, pp. 50-67.

21. In the German edition, *Hollanda*.

22. The photographs used in this edition were taken by Archivio Mas, Barcelona.

23. Identical with the painting listed in Vol. VII under No. 141, Plate 108.

24. Identical with the painting listed in Vol. VII under Add. 204, Plate 131.

25. From Vol. XIV, 1937, p. 114. This may be the picture now in the Kisters collection at Kreuzlingen (Switzerland).

26. 'It seems that this painting was lost before it came into our collections. We do not know where the painting of the *Annunciation* was lost or if it was ever found' (Statement in a letter from the Detroit Institute of Arts to the editor, 3rd August 1971).

27. Sir Martin Davies mentions two more *Adorations of the Magi*, one the centrepiece of a triptych at the National Gallery, London (No. 2155), the other in the Monasterio de las Descalzas Reales, Madrid. See Sir Martin Davies, *National Gallery Catalogues. Early Netherlandish School*, (3rd ed. London), 1968, p. 103.

28. The verso is so badly damaged that one can only speak of remnants of a *Virgin and Child with St. Anne and St. Christopher* (Letter of 2nd February 1972, from the Wallraf-Richartz-Museum, Cologne).

29. The *Christ Shown to the People* is freely copied after a woodcut in Dürer's *Small Passion* (1511). See above, p. 23.

30. The panels have now again been separated.

31. See Vol. II, No. 3, Plate 6.

32. A workshop study shows that the balcony railing seen on the window in Joos's painting in the Louvre was added at a later date. See C. Gottlieb, 'The Mystical Window in Paintings of the Salvator Mundi', in *Gazette des Beaux-Arts*, December 1960, Vol. 56, pp. 313-332.

33. We call attention to another version, now in the Ponce

Art Museum, Ponce, Puerto Rico (kindly communicated by Professor Julius S. Held).

34. There is no such *St. Jerome* in the collections of the Musées Royaux des Beaux-Arts de Belgique at Brussels. Perhaps this represents a confusion with the *St. Jerome* in half-length (Inv. No. 3035; 68,5 × 55 cm), of the same type as Friedländer's No. 40 and listed by mistake under No. 42a.

35. On the relation between the Master of the Morrison Triptych and Joos van Cleve, see W. R. Valentiner, 'Simon van Herlam, the Master of the Morrison Triptych', in *Gazette des Beaux-Arts*, Vol. 45, 1955, pp. 5-10.

36. We have not been able to identify this painting at the Staedelsches Kunstinstitut. There may be a mistake here.

37. 651, in the German edition.

38. G. Bazin has studied the Louvre version, which has the same dimensions as Friedländer's No. 55c. From the photographs, we believe that the Louvre panel cannot be either Friedländer's No. 55c or his No. 55f. See G. Bazin, 'La Donation Mège au Musée du Louvre, Departement des peintures', in *La Revue du Louvre et des Musées de France*, Vol. 11, No. 3, 1961, pp. 114 and 115.

39. The same picture was again listed by Friedländer in his Vol. XIV, 1937, p. 117, No. 4, in his catalogue of paintings by Cornelis van Cleve. (Information of 7th September 1970 from M. Cormack, Keeper of Paintings and Drawings, Fitzwilliam Museum, Cambridge).

40. This picture was not included in the sale at Christie's, 28th May 1965.

41. Vol. I, p. 62, Plate 52.

42. Mrs. Louisa Dresser, Curator of the Worcester Art Museum, states in a letter of 9th September 1970: 'This painting has never been in our collections, and Friedländer's listing as such is undoubtedly an error'.

43. Cf. also Note 35.

44. Obviously a mistake for 'Uffizi', as stated in the text.

45. 11th July 1930, No. 39.

46. Friedländer himself believed this portrait to be by Cornelis van Cleve. See M. J. Friedländer, 'Nachträgliches zu Cornelis van Cleve', in *Oud-Holland*, Vol. LX, I, 1943, pp. 8-11, ill. 5.

47. There is confusion in the German edition: Plate LII does not in fact reproduce No. 108a, but 108b, which is the Vienna rather than the Hampton Court version.

48. G. J. Hoogewerff gives this painting to Vincent Sellaer. See G. J. Hoogewerff, 'Vincent Sellaer en Zijn Verblijf te Brescia', in *Annuaire des Musées Royaux des Beaux-Arts de Belgique*, III, 1940-42, pp. 18-20.

49. I. Bengström gives a symbolic analysis of this picture. See I. Bengström, 'Disguised Symbolism in "Madonna" Pictures and Still Life. Part II', in *The Burlington Magazine*, Vol. XCVII, No. 632, November 1955, pp. 342-349.

50. In the German edition, *Libby*.

51. Identical with No 56a, listed in Vol. IX, Part I.

52. Friedländer mentions this picture in the text, p. 44, as, on the Florence art market in 1931.

53. In the museum now attributed to Lambert Lombard.

54. Vol. VII, No. 31.

55. Probably the picture listed in Vol. V, Supp. 131.

56. Vol. XII, No. 70.

57. Vol. XII, No. 71.

58. Vol. XII, No. 80.

59. See German edition, Vol. XII, p. 30, Pl. XIII.

60. Vol. XI, No. 150.

61. Vol. XI, No. 152.

62. See also Supp. 262 and Add. 273 A and 273 B.

63. For the identification of the subject see editors note.

64. Identified as St. Nicholas of Bari. See H. Pauwels, *Musée Communal des Beaux-Arts*, Bruges, 1963, pp. 62-63.

65. In the German edition, rectos.

66. Identified as St. Dominic.

66a. Cf. H. S. Leonard, 'Three Panels by Jan Provoost', in *Bulletin of the City Art Museum of St. Louis*, XXXV, 1950, pp. 49-53.

67. No. 156a is missing in the German edition. In the contemporary documents the name is spelt Jacob van den Coornhuize.

68. The versos of the triptych representing St. Anthony of Padu and St. Bonaventura, grisailles, are indeed by J. Provost.

69. For the pendant, see Add. 274.

70. On the reverse a vase with flowers in a niche.

71. Probably the picture mentioned by E. K. J. Reznicek in the collection of the Marqués de Santo Domingo at Madrid. Cf. E. K. G. Reznicek, 'De reconstructie van "t' Altaer van S. Lucas" van Maerten van Heemskerck', in *Oud-Holland*, LXX, 1955, pp. 241 and 243, fig. 7.

72. The work is here reproduced with the additions.

73. The Virgin only appears on the verso of the panel.

74. According to the *Gazette des Beaux-Arts*, LXI, April 1963, p. 4, this painting is supposed to be at the Everhart Museum, Scranton, Pa., on loan from the Anthony Geber collection.

75. Cf. J. Lavalleye, 'Collections d'Espagne,' 1 *(Les Primitifs Flamands, II. Répertoire des Peintures Flamandes des Quinzième et Seizième Siècles)*, Antwerp, 1953, p. 15, No. 11, Pl. XIII.

76. Cf. J. Lavalleye, 'Collections d'Espagne, 2' (*Les Primitifs Flamands, II. Répertoire des Peintures Flamandes des Quinzième et Seizième Siècles*), Antwerp, 1958, pp. 31-32, No. 80, Pl. XIX.

77. See L. Reis-Santos, '*Obras primas da pintura Flamenga dos seculos XV e XVI em Portugal*, Lisbon, 1953, pp. 87, 88, No. 49, Pl. XXXIX, there attributed to Quentin Massys.

78. Cf. G. Carandente, 'Collections d'Italie, 1. Sicile' (*Les Primitifs Flamands, II. Répertoire des Peintures Flamandes du Quinzième Siècle*, 3), Brussels, 1968, pp. 31-32, No. 17, Pl. XIV.

79. Now attributed by the Museum to Ulrich Apt.

80. A version in the Museés royaux des Beaux-Arts de Belgique, Brussels, Inv. No. 609; 57,7 × 43,3 cm., Perhaps No. 217c or No. 217d.

81. See Note 80.

82. Two other variant copies of the central panel mentioned by Robert A. Koch, *Joachim Patinir*, Princeton 1968, p. 75,

No. 8a (Mrs. George Kidston collection, Bristol, 31,3 × 56 cm) and No. 8b (Institute of Arts, Minneapolis, No. 14.2; 35 × 50 cm).

83. An addition 8,5 cm wide has been removed in 1954.

84. This painting is the left part of an ensemble of which the Baptism of Christ (No. 223) forms the other half. Now the two fragments have been rejoined as to form a single panel.

85. See note 84.

86. The left half of the composition appears in a panel in the Boymans-van Beuningen Museum, Rotterdam, Inv. No. 2474; 27 × 23 cm; mentioned by Robert A. Koch, *Joachim Patinir*, Princeton 1968, p. 74, No. 7. The latter suggests that this fragment and the Castagnola painting might reflect the lost original by Patenier. See also Friedländer's comments on the *Rest on the Flight into Egypt* by Joos van Cleve, listed as No. 49.

87. According to Robert A. Koch, *Joachim Patinir*, Princeton 1968, p. 79, No. 22, this picture may now be owned by Mrs. D. Hart, Jersey, Channel Islands; 112 × 111 cm. The Hart picture was included in the London 'Exhibition of Flemish and Belgian art, 1300-1900' of 1927, No. 121, as owned by Lionel Harris and came up again in 1935 at the Tomas Harris Gallery, London (No. 13, Catalogue of the Exhibition of Early Flemish Paintings—June 1935). No. 236 of Friedländer's catalogue (Vol. IX) is described as being owned in 1930 by Blumenreich in Berlin, with other dimensions, 128 × 113,5 cm.

88. Signed below towards the centre: *Joachim D Patinier*.

89. See also Sir Martin Davies, *National Gallery Catalogues. Early Netherlandish School*, (3rd ed. revised), London 1968, pp. 160, 161.

90. A repetition of this composition in the left wing and the central panel of a triptych (Principe di Trabia collection, Palermo) listed by Robert A. Koch, *Joachim Patinir*, Princeton 1968, as No. 12c and 31. See also Sir Martin Davies, *National Gallery Catalogues. Early Netherlandish School*, (3rd ed. revised), London 1968, p. 161.

91. According to Robert A. Koch, *Joachim Patinir*, Princeton 1968, p. 81, No. 28, in a private collection, Switzerland(?).

92. Slight additions have been removed from the sides and the top in 1954. We give the dimensions without the additions.

93. See also No. 127 and Add. 273A and 273B.

94. Cf. G. Carandente, 'Collections d'Italie, I. Sicile' (*Les Primitifs Flamands, II. Répertoire des Peintures Flamandes du Quinzième Siècle*, 3), Brussels, 1968, p. 42, No. 26, Pl. XIX.

95. Let us mention also the two pictures painted by Quentin Massys in collaboration with Patenier, listed in vol. VII: *Virgin and Child*, Poznan, Raczynski collection, No. 19, and *The Temptation of St. Anthony*, Madrid, Museo del Prado, No. 31.

96. See also No. 127 and Supp. 262.

97. Concerns a *Nativity* (695 × 530 mm) at the Hermitage at Leningrad, published and given to Barthel Bruyn by M. Dobroklonsky. See M. Dobroklonsky, 'Bartholomäus Bruyn (1493-1555)' in *Old Master Drawings*, XI, 1936, pp. 53-54.

98. Max J. Friedländer, 'Eine Zeichnung von Jan Joest', in *Oud-Holland*, LVII, 1940, pp. 161-167.

99. C. P. Baudisch, *Jan Joest von Kalkar. Ein Beitrag zur Kunstgeschichte des Niederrheins*. Kunstgeschichtliche Forschungen des Rheinischen Heimatbundes, Vol. 8, Bonn 1940.

100. G. J. Hoogewerff, *De Noordnederlandsche Schilderkunst*, II, The Hague, 1937, pp. 428-448.

101. A. Stange, *Deutsche Malerei der Gotik*, VI: *Nordwestdeutschland in der Zeit von 1450 bis 1515*, Munich-Berlin, 1954, pp. 63-71.

102. On this master cf. Vol. VIa, p. 44 and Vol. VIb, p. 111, Supp. 247-249; pp. 116-117, Add. 292-294.

103. This suggestion has been rejected by C. P. Baudisch, *Jan Joest von Kalkar, Ein Beitrag zur Kunstgeschichte des Niederrheins*. Kunstgeschichtliche Forschungen des Rheinischen Heimatbundes, Vol. 8, Bonn 1940, pp. 179-183.

104. In particular *The Flight into Egypt*, Munich, Bayerische Staatsgemäldesammlungen, *The Pieta*, Germany, Private collection, *The Coronation of the Virgin*, Germany, Private collection, *The Taking of Christ*, Art market.

105. *The portrait of Hans von Melem*, Munich, Alte Pinakothek, *Portrait of an Architect*, probably Laurenz Kosters, Prague, Nostiz Gallery, *Portrait of an Elderly Man*, Nuremberg, Germanisches Nationalmuseum, *Portrait of a Man* and *Portrait of a Woman* (1514), sold as 'Zeitblom' with the collection Onnes de Nyenrode, at F. Muller, Amsterdam 1933.

106. A. Stange, 'Einige Nachträge zu Jan Joest als Bildnismaler' in *Westfalen*, XXVII, 1959, pp. 236-240.

107. To the portraits already mentioned (see note 105), A. Stange adds a *Portrait of a Woman*, 35 × 24 cm, Munich, Alte Pinakothek (pendant of a *Portrait of a Man*), a *Portrait of a Young Woman*, 31 × 24 cm, Dublin, National Gallery of Ireland, and a *Portrait of an Elderly Woman*, 29.5 × 20.5 cm, formerly on the Amsterdam art market (P. de Boer).

108. J. Bruyn, 'De Abdij van Egmond als opdrachtgeefster van Kunstwerken in het begin van de zestiende eeuw. II', in *Oud-Holland*, LXXXI, 1966, p. 218.

109. E. Willemsen, 'Die Wiederherstellung der Altarflügel des Jan Joest vom Hochaltar in St. Nikolai zu Kalkar', in *Jahrbuch der Rheinischen Denkmalpflege*, XXVII, 1967, pp. 105-222.

110. Ramon Revilla Vielva, 'El tríptico de Fonseca en el Trascoro de la S. I. Catedral de Palencia', in *Publicaciones de la Institución 'Tello Téllez de Meneses'*, II, 1949, pp. 113-128; V, 1950, pp. 91-98.

111. Chandler R. Post, 'A second Retable by Jan Joest in Spain', in *Gazette des Beaux-Arts*, 6th per., XXII, 1942, pp. 127-134.

112. P. Quarré, in *Mémoires de la Commission des Antiquités de la Côte d'Or*, Vol. 25, 1959-1962, Dijon 1964, pp. 70-71.

113. Dijon, Musée des Beaux-Arts, Inv. No. 4154; 173 × 129 cm.

114. Sir Martin Davies, *National Gallery Catalogues, Early Netherlandish School*, (3rd ed. revised), London, 1968, p. 69; E. Panofsky, *Early Netherlandish Painting. Its Origins and Character*, 2nd ed., Cambridge, Mass., 1958, p. 354.

115. H. Gerson, 'Joos van Cleve', in *Mededelingen van het*

Rijksbureau voor Kunsthistorische Documentatie, in *Oud-Holland*, LXX, 1955, pp. 129-131.

115a. J. Białostocki, 'Joos van Cleve in dem Kalkarer Altar', in *Kunsthistorische Forschungen Otto Pächt zu seinem 70. Geburtstag*, Salzburg, 1972, pp. 189-195. The various opinions concerning the formation of van Cleve are listed in this publication.

116. W. R. Valentiner, 'Simon van Herlam, the Master of the Morrison Triptych', in *Gazette des Beaux-Arts*, 6th per., XLV, 1955, pp. 5-10.

117. G. J. Hoogewerff, 'Vincent Sellaer en zijn verblijf te Brescia', in *Annuaire des Musées royaux des Beaux-Arts de Belgique*, III, 1940-1942, p. 20.

118. *Idem*, 'Pittori fiamminghi in Liguria nel secolo XVI', in *Commentari*, XII, 1961, pp. 185-191.

119. G. Marlier, 'Joos van Cleve—Fontainebleau and Italy', in *The Connoisseur*, CLXV, may 1967, pp. 24-27.

120. E. P. Richardson, 'The Adoration of the Magi by J. van Cleve', in *The Art Quarterly*, IX, 1946, pp. 182-186.

121. J. Białostocki, 'Nieznane Autoportrety Joosa Van Cleve Przyczynki do Twórczosci Mistrza ze Zbiorów Polskich', in *Biuletyn historii sztuki*, XVI, 1954, pp. 464-468; *Idem*, 'New Observations on Joos van Cleve', in *Mededelingen van het Rijksbureau voor Kunsthistorische Documentatie*, in *Oud-Holland*, LXX, 1955, pp. 121-129; *Idem*, 'Gdańskie Dzieło Joosa van Cleve. Z Dziejów Artystycznych Stosunków Gdańska z Niderlandami', in *Studia Pomorskie*, I, 1957, pp. 170-230.

122. J. Białostocki, 'New Observations...', *op. cit.*, p. 125. According to R. A. Koch, *Joachim Patenir*, Princeton, 1968, pp. 52-54 nothing authorizes to think that the two painters have met in Bruges.

123. J. Snyder, 'St. John on Patmos by Joos van Cleve', in *The University of Michigan Museum of Art Bulletin*, new series, II, 1966-1967, pp. 9-12.

124. I. Bergström, 'Disguised Symbolism in "Madonna" Pictures and Still-Life', in *The Burlington Magazine*, XCVII, 1955, pp. 303-308; 342-349.

125. C. G. Stridbeck, 'Den gåtfulla nejlikan. Några reflektioner kring ett aktuellt ikonologiskt motiv', in *Konsthistorisk Tidskrift*, XXIX, 1960, pp. 81-97.

126. J. Hand, *Joos van Cleve and the Saint Jerome in the Norton Gallery and School of Art*. Norton Gallery Studies. I, West Palm Beach, 1972.

127. H. Gerson, 'Joos van Cleve', *loc. cit.*

128. J. Rosenberg, 'Early Flemish Painting', in *The Bulletin of the Fogg Museum of Art*, X, 1943, p. 48.

129. The author, however, does not state if this identification is based on the coats of arms.

129a. S. Bergmans, 'De Quelques Portraits Inconnus de Sir Thomas Wyat le Jeune et de Leur Attribution', in *Apollo*, Brussels, Septembre 1941, No. 4, pp. 8-11.

130. A. Staring, 'Vraagstukken der Oranje-Iconographie. II. Rond twee portretten van Jan Gossaert van Mabuse', in *Oud-Holland*, LXVII, 1952, pp. 151-156.

131. Besides the versions listed by Friedländer, we wish to mention two more replicas: 1) The Hague, 'Koninklijk Huisarchief', tondo, diam. 62 cm. See A. Staring, *op. cit.*, pp. 153-154, plate 8. 2) Gaasbeek, Collections du Château-Musée, 74.5 × 58.5 cm. See G. Renson and M. Casteels, 'Prospections dans les collections du Château-Musée de Gaasbeek', in *Le Folklore Brabançon*, No. 170, juin 1966, pp. 140-141.

132. Vol. VIII, No. 55 and p. 115.

133. See also Add. No. 272.

134. From the church of the Certosini at Melegnano (Lombardy). About 1920 the centrepiece was in the Chiesa collection in Milan. G. J. Hoogewerff, 'Pittori fiamminghi in Liguria nel secolo XVI', in *Commentari*, XII, 1961, p. 188.

135. 123.8 × 86.4 cm., New York, Metropolitan Museum of Art. Acc. No. 40.174.1. Cf. M. Salinger, 'Two New Flemish Paintings', in *Bulletin of the Metropolitan Museum of Art*, XXXVI, 1941, pp. 109-111.

136. 34 × 27 cm, Paris, private collection. G. Marlier, 'Joos van Cleve-Fontainebleau and Italy', in *The Connoisseur* CLXV, May 1967, p. 27. An other specimen of the type No. 36.

137. 72.5 × 54 cm, Brussels, Musées royaux des Beaux-Arts de Belgique, Inv. No. 7224. G. Marlier, *op. cit.*, p. 26. Another specimen of the type is No. 37.

138. 68.9 × 51.4 cm, West Palm Beach, Norton Gallery and School of Art. Published as 'workshop of Joos van Cleve', by J. Hand, *loc. cit.* Another specimen of the type No. 40.

139. Cambridge, Mass., Busch-Reisinger Museum, Harvard University. Cf. J. Hand, *op.cit.*

140. 89 × 69.6 cm, Prague, Narodní Galerie. J. Šip, 'Novy Obraz Joose Van Cleve', in *Umění*, I, 1953, pp. 134-140. An other specimen of the type No. 114.

141. 43 × 31.5 cm, San Francisco, Calif., The California Palace of the Legion of Honor, No. 1948.5. J. D. P., 'Francis I. Patron of the Arts', in *Bulletin of the California Palace of the Legion of Honor*, VI, 1948, pp. 22-27. The second portrait painted on copper 17.4 × 13.3 cm, Berlin, Kunstbibliothek. E. Berckenhagen, 'Ein von Joos van Cleve signiertes (?) Portrait König Franz' I.', in *Berliner Museen*, new series, XV, 1965, pp. 12-14. According to J. G. van Gelder, 'Zu "Ein von Joos van Cleve signiertes (?) Portrait König Franz I." ', *ibid.* p. 57, the monogram appearing on this portrait must be considered as that of Lucas Horenhout.

141a. The painting No. C. 26 (Vol. IXa, p. 74) is now in the Koninklijk Museum voor Schone Kunsten, Antwerp, No. 5037; 60 × 73 cm, as 'Master of St. Sebastian'.

142. Max J. Friedländer, 'Nachträgliches zu Cornelis van Cleve', in *Oud-Holland*, LX, 1943, pp. 7-14.

143. It is worth noting that in this article Friedländer gives the *Adoration of the Christ Child*, from the Dresden Museum back to Joos van Cleve, after having listed it in his Vol. XIV among the works by Cornelis (see Vol. IXa, p. 72, No. C.1).

144. 52.1 × 88.9 cm, Enschede (Netherlands), Mrs. C. F. L. van Heek collection. E. P. Richardson, 'Pierre Samuel du Pont de Nemours as a collector', in *The Art Quarterly*, XXXII, 1969, p. 50.

145. 27.6 × 19.3 cm, Detroit, Mich., Institute of Arts. E. P.

Richardson. 'A Madonna by Cornelis van Cleve', in *Bulletin of the Detroit Institute of Arts*, XVIII, 1938-39, No. 2, p. 2.

146. 109 × 83 cm, Leningrad, The Hermitage, Inv. 2350. E. Fechner, 'Ein neuaufgefundenes Bild des Cornelis van Cleve', in *Musée de l'Ermitage. Travaux du Département de l'Art Européen*, I, 1940, pp. 92-96 and 97. This author is tempted to give to Cornelis van Cleve some late portraits from the œuvre of Joos van Cleve which from their style may be dated roundabout 1550.

147. S. Bergmans, 'De Quelques portraits inconnus de Sir Thomas Wyat le Jeune et de leur attribution', in *Apollo* (Brussels), No. 4, 1 sept. 1941, pp. 8-11. Let us mention that S. Bergmans expresses some doubts concerning the identification of 'Sotte Cleef' with Cornelis van Cleve.

148. R. Parmentier, 'Bronnen voor de Geschiedenis van het Brugsche Schildersmilieu in de XVe eeuw. XIX. Jan Provost', in *Revue belge d'Archéologie et d'Histoire de l'Art*, XI, 1941, pp. 97-118.

149. F. Bologna, 'Nuove Attribuzioni a Jan Provost', in *Musées royaux des Beaux-Arts [de Belgique]. Bulletin*, V, 1956, pp. 13-31.

150. F. Bologna, 'Nuove Attribuzioni...', *op. cit.*, pp. 36-37, suggests also that J. Provost may have sojourned in Portugal, especially between 1501 and 1507.

151. S. Speth-Holterhoff, 'Trois panneaux de Jean Provost', in *Musées royaux des Beaux-Arts de Belgique. Bulletin*, XIV, 1965, pp. 15-17.

152. C. L. Ragghianti, 'Sull' opera di Jan Provost', in *La Critica d'Arte*, XXX, 1949-50, pp. 334-337.

153. G. J. Hoogewerff, 'Pittori fiamminghi in Liguria nel secolo XVI', in *Commentari*, XII, 1961, pp. 183-184.

154. F. J. Sanchez Cantón, 'La reconstrucción de un políptico de Jan Provost', in *Miscellanea Prof. Dr. D. Roggen*, Antwerp, 1957, pp. 249-255.

155. P. Pieper, 'Zu einem Sippenaltar von Jan Provost', in *Festschrift G. Fiensch.* (Giessener Beiträge zur Kunstgeschichte, I), 1970, pp. 51-60.

156. 32 × 26 cm.

157. According to P. Pieper, the Louvre panel does not represent Emerence but Humerie.

158. G. Ring, 'Additions to the Work of Jan Provost and Quentin Massys. I. Jan Provost: A Series of Panels from his Early Period', in *The Burlington Magazine*, LXXIX, 1941, pp. 156-160.

159. G. Ring suggests, without verification, since she does not know the dimensions, that the three panels with scenes of the *Passion of Christ* (No. 138) may come from the same ensemble.

160. *Museum Boymans-van Beuningen Rotterdam. Catalogus Schilderijen tot 1800*, Rotterdam, 1962, p. 106.

161. N. Verhaegen, 'Revers de volets peints révélés par radiographie', in *Bulletin de l'Institut royal du Patrimoine Artistique*, I, 1958, pp. 92-102.

162. A. Janssens de Bisthoven, 'De Herstelling van het Laatste Oordeel van Jan Provoost', in *Gentse Bijdragen tot de Kunstgeschiedenis en de Oudheidkunde*, XVII, 1957-58, pp. 123-133.

163. J. Marrow, 'John the Baptist, Lantern for the Lord: New Attributes for the Baptist from the Northern Netherlands', in *Oud-Holland*, LXXXIII, 1968, p. 4.

164. Nettuno, Principe de Cassaro collection. F. Bologna, 'Nuove attribuzioni a Jan Provost', in *Musées royaux des Beaux-Arts [de Belgique]. Bulletin*, V, 1956, pp. 13-20.

165. Bergamo, Galleria della Accademia Carrara. *Idem*, 'Nuove attribuzioni...', *op. cit.*, p. 30.

166. 18 × 15 cm, Madrid, Museo del Prado, N. 2696. S. Sulzberger, 'Une Vierge de Jan Provost au Musée du Prado?', in *Mededelingen van het Rijksbureau voor Kunsthistorische Documentatie*, in *Oud-Holland*, LXXVI, 1961, p. 107. The attribution is put forward as a supposition.

167. Reggio Emilia, Museo Parmeggiani. C. L. Ragghianti, 'Sull' opera di Jan Provost', in *La Critica d'Arte*, XXX, 1949-50, p. 337.

168. 49 × 37.5 cm, Palermo, Amedeo Chiaramonte Bordonaro di Gebbiarossa collection, Inv. No. 105. G. Carandente, 'Collections d'Italie. I. Sicile' (*Les Primitifs flamands. II. Répertoire des Peintures flamandes du quinzième siècle*), Brussels, 1968, p. 12, No. 4.

169. 29.3 × 20.4 cm, Madrid, Noguès collection. J. Lavalleye, 'Collections d'Espagne'. 2. (*Les Primitifs flamands. II. Répertoire des quinzième et seizième siècles*), Antwerp, 1958, pp. 34-35, No. 84.

170. 84 × 71 cm, Douai, Musée, No. 408. S. Speth-Holterhoff, 'Trois panneaux de Jean Provost' in *Musées royaux des Beaux-Arts de Belgique. Bulletin*, XIV, 1965, p. 19. This attribution is put forward by the author as a supposition. The painting is listed by Friedländer in the catalogue of Jean Bellegambe, vol. XII, No. 130.

171. *Anonieme Vlaamse Primitieven. Zuidnederlandse Meesters met Noodnamen van de 15de en het begin van de 16de Eeuw*, Bruges, 1969, pp. 68-87, 219-233.

172. Sir Martin Davies, *National Gallery Catalogues. Early Netherlandish School*, London, 1945, p. 65; idem, (3rd ed. revised), London, 1968, p. 99; C. Ragghianti, 'Il Maestro delle "Scene della Passione" di Bruges', in *La Critica d'Arte*, XXX, 1949, p. 340.

173. C. Ragghianti, 'Il Maestro delle "Scene della Passione" ...', *op. cit.*, pp. 338-340; [C.] R[agghianti], 'Disegni fiamminghi e olandesi agli Uffizi', in *La Critica d'Arte*, XII, N.S., 1965, pp. 7, 8.

174. Concerning the Master of the Turin Adoration, cf. Vol. VIb, pp. 44, 111 (Supp. 250), 117 (Add. 295-296), 125.

175. H. Demoriane, 'Le Maître de 1500', in *Connaissance des Arts*, No. 208, june 1969, pp. 72-79, 162.

176. Sir Martin Davies, 'The National Gallery, London' (*Les Primitifs Flamands. I. Corpus de la Peinture des Anciens Pays-Bas Méridionaux au Quinzième Siècle*, 3), II, Antwerp, 1954, pp. 199-202.

177. Ch. P. Parkhurst, 'The Madonna of the Writing Christ Child', in *The Art Bulletin*, XXIII, 1941, p. 296. Cf. also J.

Squilbeck, 'La Vierge à l'Encrier ou à l'Enfant écrivant', in *Revue belge d'Archéologie et d'Histoire de l'Art*, XIX, 1950, pp. 127-140.

178. 63.2 × 38.7 cm, New York, Wrightsman collection. Cf. E. Fahy, 'A Madonna by Gerard David', in *Apollo*, XC, sept. 1969, pp. 190-192.

179. D. Schubert, 'Halbfigurige Lucretia-Tafeln der 1. Hälfte des 16. Jahrhunderts in den Niederlanden', in *Kunsthistorisches Jahrbuch der Universität Graz*, VI, 1971, p. 102.

For this subject see also : V. Bruncel, 'Une Lucrèce du Maître du Saint-Sang', in *Les Beaux-Arts* (Brussels), No. 783, 18 oct. 1957, p. 8.

180. H. Schwarz, 'The Mirror of the Artist and the Mirror of the Devout' in *Studies in the History of Art dedicated to William E. Suida on His Eightieth Birthday*, New York, 1959, p. 94.

181. M. J. Friedländer, *Essays über die Landschaftsmalerei und andere Bildgattungen*, The Hague, 1947, pp. 54-67. On pp. 61-62 the author enumerates Patenier's principal paintings, including two pairs of pendants of 'pure Landscape', one on the art market in Amsterdam, the other in a private collection in Germany. It has not been possible to trace these panels, two of which seem to correspond to Supp. 269 and 270.

182. R. A. Koch, *Joachim Patinir* (Princeton Monographs in Art and Archaeology, No. 38,) Princeton, 1968. The main lines of Koch's thesis were taken over by J. Combs Stuebe, in 'Landscape with the Flight into Egypt : Patinir or the Master of the Half-Lengths'? in *North Carolina Museum of Art Bulletin*, Vol. X, No. 2, Dec. 1970, pp. 3-12. Among the reviews of the work of Koch, we cite: Ch. D. Cuttler and B. L. Dunbar, in 'Art Quarterly', vol. 32, 1969, pp. 431-433 ; J. Bruyn, in 'Oud-Holland', vol. 85, 1970, p. 141 ; D. Schubert, in 'Kunstchronik', vol. 24, 1971, pp. 73-77 ; K. G. Boon, in 'The Art Bulletin', vol. 55, 1973, pp. 297-298.

182a. Let us point out that R. A. Koch, *op. cit.*, pp. 14, 15, expresses some doubt about G. David's influence on Patenier's formation, but sees already in the earliest work that of J. Bosch.

183. For the *catalogue critique* see R. A. Koch, *Joachim Patinir, op. cit.*, pp. 70-89. The author lists the differences between this catalogue and Friedländer's on p. 21, note 14, and p. 57, note 6.

184. A. Piron, *La peinture wallonne ancienne*, Gilly, 1963, pp. 59-64 ; *Idem, Joachim le Patinier, Henri Blès*, Gembloux, 1971, pp. 11-28 ; *Idem*, 'Nouvelles recherches Concernant les peintres Joachim le Patinier et Henri Bles', in *La nouvelle Revue Wallonne*, XIV, 1964, pp. 101-112, 157-164.

185. Ed. Gérard, 'Les paysagistes Patenier et Henri de Bouvigne', in *Communications du XXXVIIe Congrès de la Fédération archéologique et historique de Belgique*, Brussels, 1958, p. 26 ; *Idem, Dinant und die Maas in der Geschichte der Landschaftsmalerei. Dinant et la Meuse dans l'Histoire du Paysage*, Lammersdorf, 1960, pp. 23-32. In a chapter of this book devoted to Patenier, the author provides, pp. 95-105, a catalogue of the works he believes to be by the painter.

186. A. Barret, 'Patinir : au crépuscule du moyen âge un élève de Jérome Bosch invente de fantastiques panoramas', in *Connaissance des Arts*, No. CX, Dec. 1967, pp. 94-103, 127-129.

187. M. Kunel, 'Joachim Patenier au Musée du Prado', in *Le Cahier des Arts*, Vol. VII, 1962, pp. 2757-2760 ; Vol. 9, 1964, p. 3300.

188. C. Van de Wetering, *Die Entwicklung der niederländischen Landschaftsmalerei vom Anfang des 16. Jahrhunderts bis zur Jahrhundertmitte*, Berlin, 1938, pp. 24-30.

189. G. J. Hoogewerff, *Het landschap van Bosch tot Rubens*, Antwerp, 1954, pp. 17-27.

190. G. Künstler, 'Landschaftsdarstellung und religiöses Weltbild in der Tafelmalerei der Übergangsepoche um 1500' in *Jahrbuch der Kunsthistorischen Sammlungen in Wien*, Vol. LXII, 1966, pp. 121-128.

191. H. G. Franz, *Niederländische Landschaftsmalerei im Zeitalter des Manierismus*, Graz, 1969, pp. 29-49.

192. F. M. Godfrey, 'The Baptism of Christ in Flemish Painting and Miniature from Roger van der Weyden to Patinier', in *Apollo*, Vol. LII, 1950, pp. 132-134. This author stresses mainly Patenier's feeling for landscape as it developed around the theme of the *Baptism of Christ*.

193. Å. Bengtsson, 'A Painting by Joachim Patinir', in *Idea and Form. Studies in the History of Art. Acta Universitatis Upsaliensis*. Vol. I, (new series), 1959, pp. 88-94.

194. R. A. Koch, in *Joachim Patinir, loc. cit.*, p. 87, on the other hand, attributes this painting to the Master of the Female Half-Lengths.

195. A. Dupont, 'Une vue de Namur dans un paysage de Patenier au Musée du Prado', in Namurcum, Vol. XXXVII, No. 2, 1965, pp. 21-25.

196. R. A. Koch, 'La Sainte-Baume in Flemish Landscape Painting of the Sixteenth Century', in *Gazette des Beaux-Arts*, 6th period, Vol. LXVI, 1965, pp. 273-282.

197. According to R. A. Koch, in *Joachim Patinir, op. cit.*, p. 76, the title *The Ecstasy of Mary Magdalen* seems more appropriated than *The Assumption of the Egyptian Mary* adopted by Friedländer.

198. A third painting, *St. Jerome in the Wilderness*, Antwerp, Mayer van den Bergh Museum, Cat. No. 367; 17,3 cm in diameter, shows the same site. See R. A. Koch, *Joachim Patinir, op. cit.*, p. 82, No. 29. Koch regards this as a workshop product. The painting is not listed in Friedländer's catalogue.

199. G. J. Hoogewerff, *Het Landschap van Bosch tot Rubens, op. cit.*, p. 26. This author first formulated this hypotheses in his article, 'Joachim Patinir en Italie', in *La Revue de l'Art*, Vol. XLV, 1928, pp. 117-134.

200. R. A. Koch, 'La Sainte-Baume...', *op. cit.*, pp. 278-279.

201. Å. Bengtsson, 'A Painting by Patinir', *op. cit.*, p. 91.

202. N. Nikulin, 'Paysage avec le "Repos de la Sainte Famille en Egypte", attribué à Patinier', in *Bulletin of the Hermitage*, Vol. XX, 1961, pp. 14-16.

203. J. R. Teixeira Leite, 'O "Repouso durante a Fuga para o Egito" do Museu Nacional de Belas Artes', in *Boletim do Museu Nacional de Belas Artes*, Oct. 1962, pp. 19-20.

204. 'A Very Early Landscape', in *Museum News. The Toledo Museum of Art.*, Vol. LXXXVI, 1939, pp. 8-9.

Index of Places

J.J. = Jan Joest
Joos = Joos van Cleve
C. = Cornelis van Cleve
Pr. = Provost
B.M. 1500 = Bruges Master of 1500
M.A.M. = Master of the André Madonna
M.S.S. = Master of St. Sang
Pa. = Patenier
c. = copy

Numbers refer to the Catalogues, unless stated differently.

Plates

PHOTOGRAPHS

Unless listed below, photos were supplied by the museums, institutions or collectors owning the works. Numbers within brackets refer to the catalogues.

M. Abel-Menne, Wuppertal-Elberfeld: Plate 232 (243)
A.C.L., Brussels: Plates 137, 138, 139, 144, 145, 147, 152, 153, 154, 157, 170, 173, 174, 175, 180 (172), 187, 189, 194, 197, 198, 199, 202 (201), 204 (208), 205 (211), 213 (220a), 220, 222, 229 (241), 235, 236, 237, 239 (248)
Alinari, Florence: Plates 178 (166), 238 (245a)
Annan, Glasgow: Plate 180 (169)
P. Bijtebier, Brussels: Plates 172 (159), 243 (255)
Blinkhorn-Haynes, Banbury: Plates 164 (142), 185 (179)
Brunel, Lugano: Plates 186 (181), 190 (188), 221, 247
A. Dingjan, The Hague: Plates 140, 141
U. Edelmann, Frankfurt/M.: Plate 205 (213)
A. Frequin, The Hague: Plates 148 (127), 156, 211 (219)
Hossfeld, Darmstadt: Plate 181 (174)
R. Kleinhempel, Hamburg: Plates 172 (158), 196 (194), 204 (210)
Manzotti, Piacenza: Plate 178 (167)
Mas, Barcelona: Plate 166 (146)
A. Mewbourn, Houston: Plate 202 (203)
Ministério da Educação National, Direcção-Geral do Ensino Superior e das Belas Artes, Lisbon: Plates 142, 143
Musées Nationaux, Versailles: Plates 151 (129), 185 (180), 238 (245)
Piaget studio, St. Louis: Plate 163
R.K.D., The Hague: Plates 11 (3), (4a), (4b), 12(6), 31(15a), 46(24), 49(27a), (27b), 51(29), 53(33), (A), 54, 56(38c), 57 (40c), 58(42), 59(44), 60(45a), (45b), 61(46), (46a), 65(51), 66(52), 68(54), 69, 70(55a), (55b), (55e), (55f), (55i), 71(56b), (56d), 72(57a), 74(59b), 76(61), 79(63e), (63i), 81(64b), (64d), (64e), 82(65b), 84(66d), 94(75), 95(76), (77), 97, 99, 105(91a), (91b), 106(92), 108(97), 111(102), (103), (104), 112(107), 115(108h), 116(109a), (110), 117(112), 124(116b), 128(A), (B), 132(C. 14), 148(127), 149(127), 155(130), 164 (139), (141), 167(148), (150), 168(153), 177(162), (164), (165), 185(179), 190(189), 191, 195, 202(202), 203, 206(214), (214a), 207(217a), 208, 209, 210, 212, 213(220b), 217(225), 219(227a), 234(242), 239(247), (249), 241(252), 244, 248, 249 (Supp. 265), 252 (Supp. 269)
A. G. Schwitters, Basle: Plate 186(183)
W. Steinkopf, Berlin-Dahlem: Plates 166(144), 226, 227
Vaghi, Parma: Plate 150
A. Villani, Bologna: Plates 160, 161, 165

121. J. Provost. Altarpiece of the Virgin Enthroned. *Hampton Court, Royal Collections*

121. J. Provost. Altarpiece of the Virgin Enthroned, Centrepiece. *Hampton Court, Royal Collections*

Plate
139

121. J. Provost. Altarpiece of the Virgin Enthroned, Shutters, Donor with St. John the Baptist and Donatrix with St. Barbara (?). *Hampton Court, Royal Collections*

Plate
140

122. J. Provost. Altarpiece of the Virgin and Child. *The Hague, Koninklijk Kabinet van Schilderijen, Mauritshuis, on loan from the Rijksmuseum, Amsterdam*

122. J. Provost. Altarpiece of the Virgin and Child, Centrepiece. *The Hague, Koninklijk Kabinet van Schilderijen, Mauritshuis, on loan from the Rijksmuseum, Amsterdam*

Plate 142

123. J. Provost. Altarpiece of the Virgin Enthroned. *Lisbon, Museu Nacional de Arte Antiga*

Plate 143

123. J. Provost. Altarpiece of the Virgin Enthroned, Centrepiece. *Lisbon, Museu Nacional de Arte Antiga*

Plate
144

124. J. Provost. Altarpiece of the Adoration of the Magi. *Stourhead, Wiltshire (National Trust)*

124. J. Provost. Altarpiece of the Adoration of the Magi, Centrepiece. *Stourhead, Wiltshire (National Trust)*

Plate 146

125. J. Provost. Altarpiece of the Adoration of the Magi. *Zurich, Kunsthaus, Leopold Ruzicka-Stiftung*

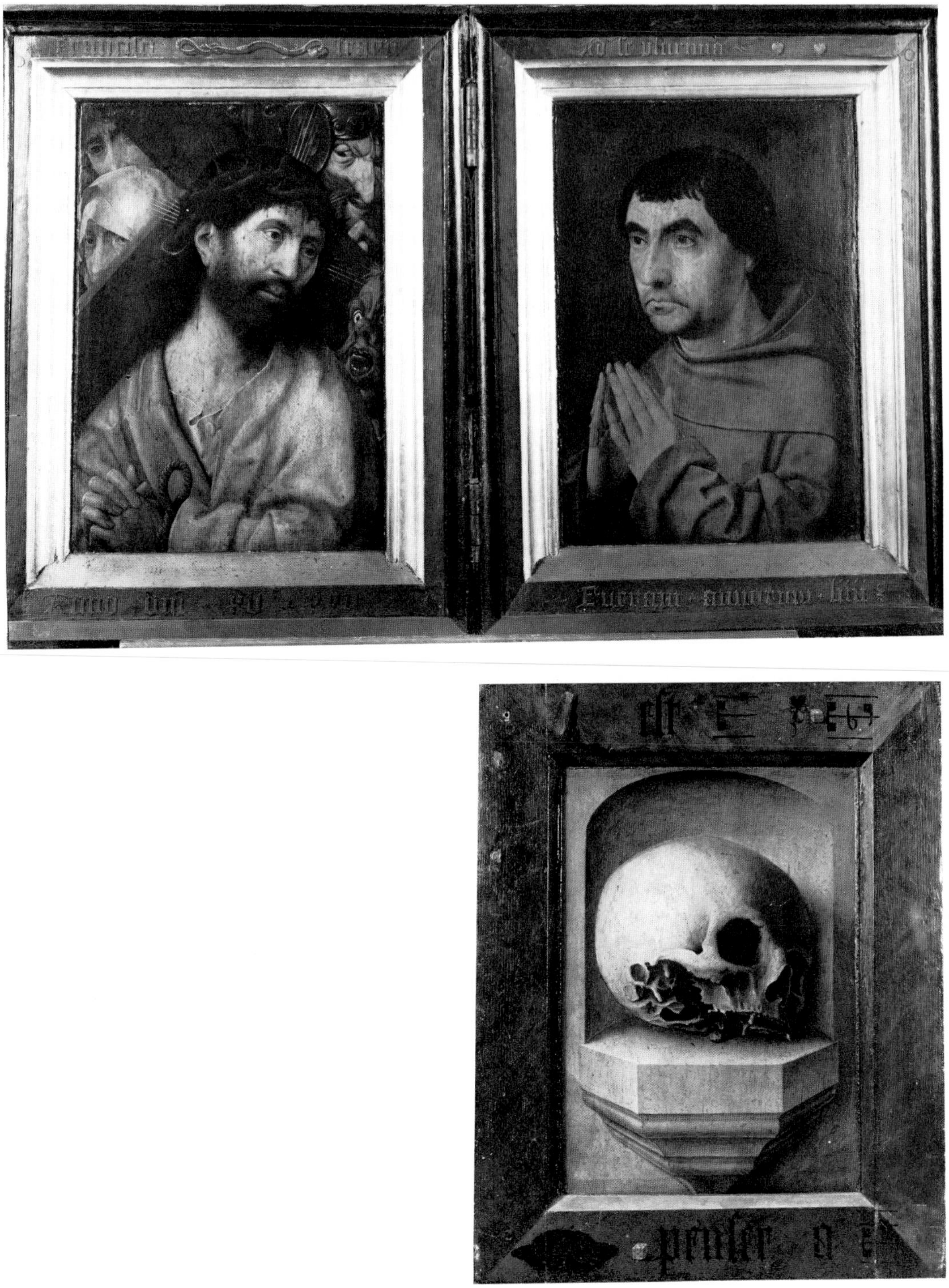

126. J. Provost. Diptych, Christ Carrying the Cross, A Monk-Donor, with Reverse. *Bruges, St. John's Hospital*

Plate
148

Supp. 262 | 127 | 127

J. Provost. Altarpiece Panels. Supp. 262. Birth of the Virgin. *Present location unknown*. 127. Annunciation. *Rotterdam, Museum Boymans-van Beuningen*. 127. Nativity. *Present location unknown*

Plate
149

Add. 273 A | 127

J. Provost. Altarpiece Panels. Add. 273 A. Presentation in the Temple. *Laren, Prof. H.J. Hellema collection.* 127. Christ Appearing to His Mother. *Present location unknown*

128. J. Provost. A Pair of Shutters, St. John the Baptist, St. Jerome. *Parma, Galleria Nazionale, Palazzo della Pilotta*

Plate 151

129. J. Provost. A Pair of Shutters, Emerence, with Reverse. *Paris, Musée du Louvre*. Zachary, with Reverse. *Madrid, Museo del Prado*

Plate
152

132. J. Provost. A Pair of Shutters, Left Shutter: Donor with St. Nicholas. *Bruges, Stedelijk Museum voor Schone Kunsten (Groeninge Museum)*

132. J. Provost. A Pair of Shutters, Right Shutter: Donatrix with St. Godelieve. *Bruges, Stedelijk Museum voor Schone Kunsten (Groeninge Museum)*

133. J. Provost. A Pair of Shutters, Death and the Miser. *Bruges, Stedelijk Museum voor Schone Kunsten (Groeninge Museum)*

131 | 130

131. J. Provost. A Pair of Shutters, St. Catherine, Female Saint. *Wassenaar, Netherlands, Mrs. J. van Stolk-Carp collection.*
130. J. Provost. A Pair of Shutters, Shepherds, Two Women. *Present location unknown*

Plate
156

135. J. Provost. A Pair of Shutters, Legend of St. Catherine: Disputation of the Saint, with Reverse. *Rotterdam, Museum Boymans-van Beuningen*

135. J. Provost. A Pair of Shutters, Legend of St. Catherine: Beheading of the Saint, with Reverse. *Antwerp, Koninklijk Museum voor Schone Kunsten*

Plate
158

134
136

134. J. Provost. A Pair of Shutters, Donor with St. Andrew, Donatrix with St. Catherine, with Reverses, Annunciation. *Philadelphia, Pa., John G. Johnson Collection.* 136. J. Provost. A Pair of Shutters, John the Baptist, St. Dominic. *Enschede, Rijksmuseum Twenthe*

134. J. Provost. A Pair of Shutters, Donor with St. Andrew, Donatrix with St. Catherine. *Philadelphia, Pa., John G. Johnson Collection*

Plate
160

137. J. Provost. A Pair of Shutters, Left Shutter: St. Peter. *Genoa, Palazzo Bianco, on loan from the Civil Hospital*

137. J. Provost. A Pair of Shutters, Right Shutter: St. Elizabeth. *Genoa, Palazzo Bianco, on loan from the Civil Hospital*

Plate
162

138. J. Provost. Three Altarpiece Panels, Scourging of Christ, Christ on the Cross, Lamentation. *St. Louis, Mo., St. Louis Art Museum*

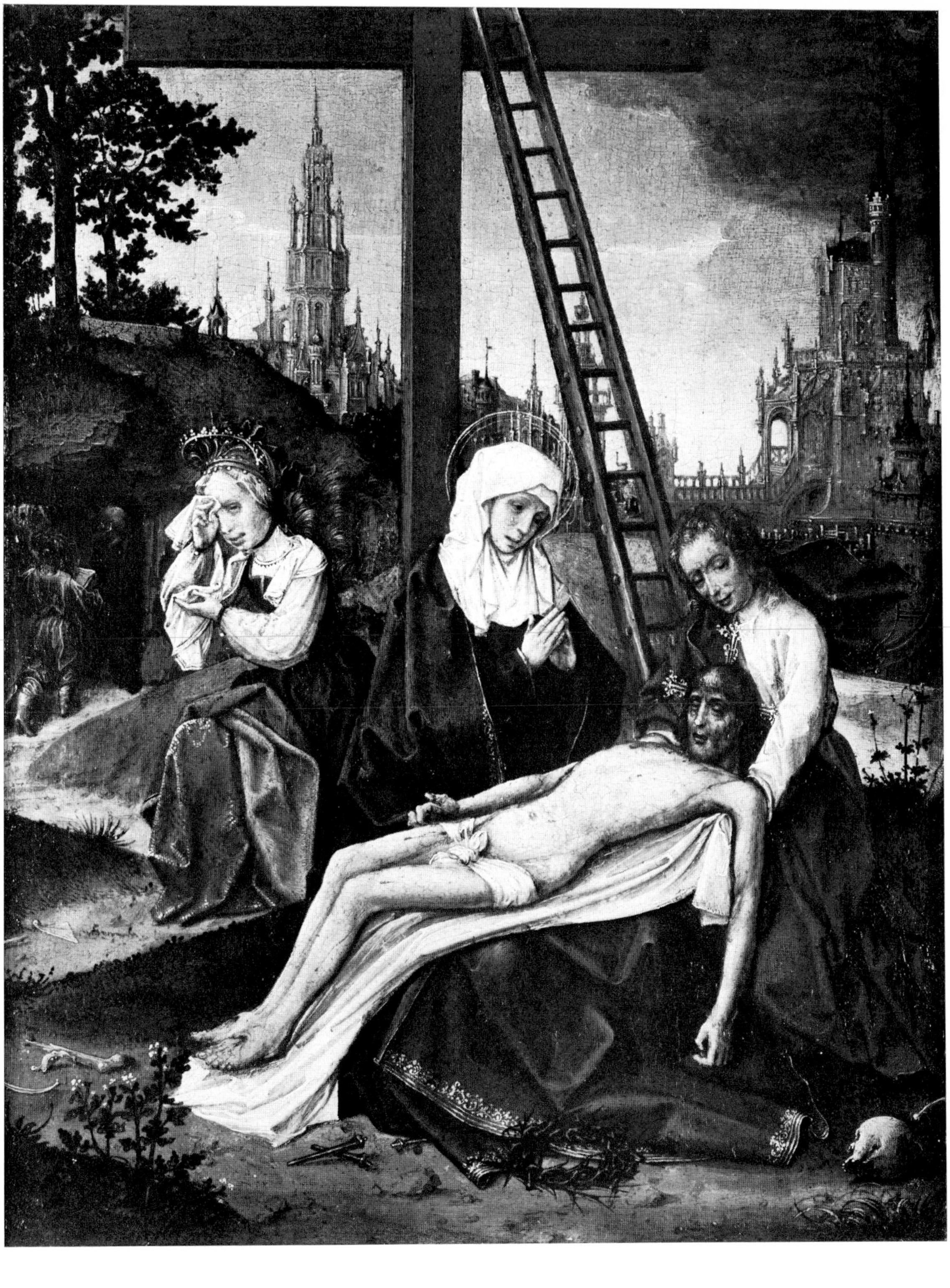

138. J. Provost. Lamentation. *St. Louis, Mo., St. Louis Art Museum*

Plate
164

139	142
141

139. J. Provost. Abraham and the Angel. *Present location unknown.* 141. J. Provost. Annunciation. *Great-Britain, Sir B.S. Barlow collection.* 142. J. Provost. Nativity. *Banbury, Upton House (National Trust)*

140. J. Provost. Annunciation. *Genoa, Palazzo Bianco, on loan from the Civil Hospital*

Plate
166

143 | 144
146

143. J. Provost. Nativity. *Amsterdam, Mrs. H.A. Wetzlar collection.* 144. J. Provost. Adoration of the Magi. *Berlin-Dahlem, Gemäldegalerie der Staatlichen Museen.* 146. J. Provost. Baptism of Christ. *Guadalupe, Convent*

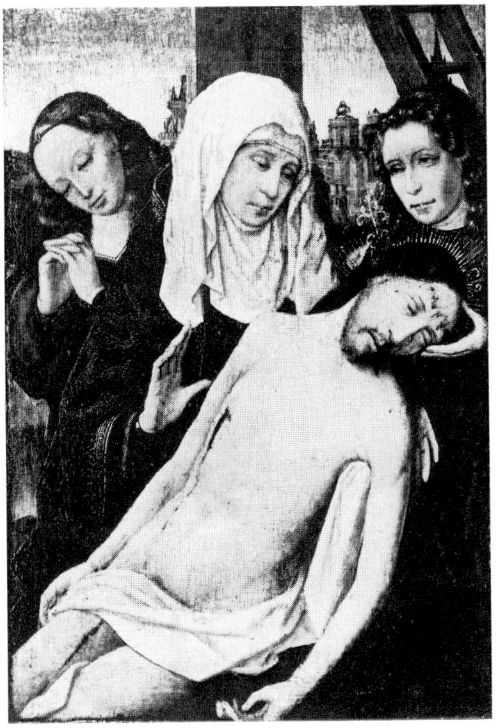

147 | 148
150 | 151

147. J. Provost. Christ Carrying the Cross. *Cologne, Lempertz auction*, 1970. 148. J. Provost. Christ Carrying the Cross. *Present location unknown*. 150. J. Provost. Lamentation. Present location unknown. 151. J. Provost. Lamentation. *Zurich, Dr. H.C. Walter Boveri collection*

Plate
168

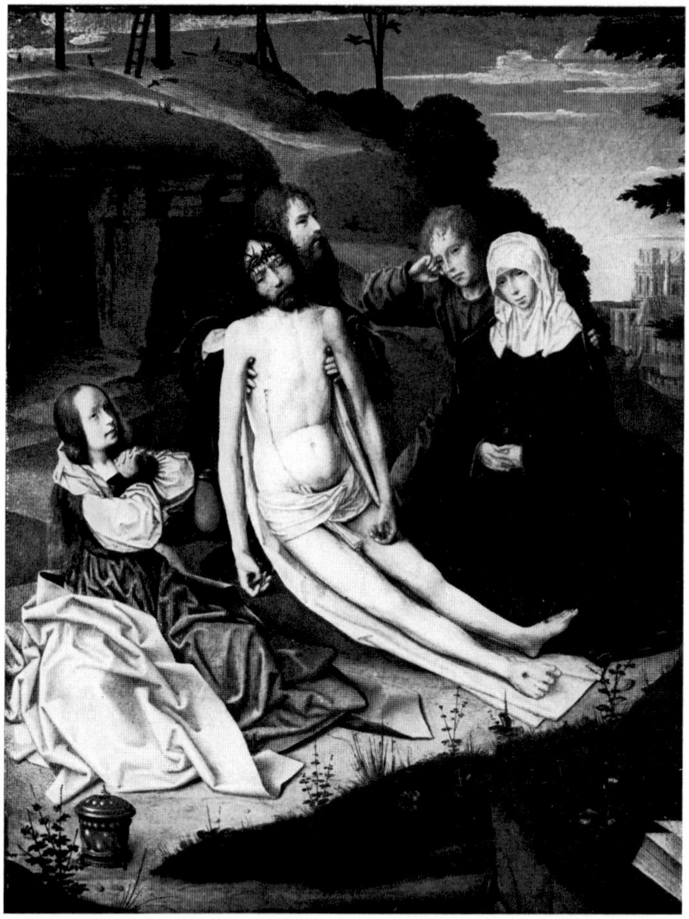

152 | 153

154 | 155

152. J. Provost. Lamentation. *Williamstown, Mass., Sterling and Francine Clark Art Institute.* 153. J. Provost. Entombment. *Present location unknown.* 154. J. Provost. Entombment. *Frankfurt, Staedelsches Kunstinstitut.* 155. J. Provost. Resurrection. *Winterthur, O. Reinhardt collection*

156. J. Provost. The Last Judgment. *Bruges, Stedelijk Museum voor Schone Kunsten (Groeninge Museum)*

Plate
170

156 b. J. Provost, Copy by J. van den Coornhuuze. The Last Judgment. *Bruges, Stedelijk Museum voor Schone Kunsten (Groeninge Museum)*

157. J. Provost. The Last Judgment. *Detroit, Mich., Institute of Arts*

Plate 172

158
———
159

158. J. Provost. The Last Judgment. *Hamburg, Kunsthalle.*
159. J. Provost. The Last Judgment. *Luxembourg, Private collection*

160. J. Provost. Altarpiece of the Legends of St. Anthony of Padua and St. Bonaventure.
Brussels, Musées Royaux des Beaux-Arts de Belgique

Plate
174

160. J. Provost. Altarpiece of the Legends of St. Anthony of Padua and St. Bonaventure, Centrepiece.
Brussels, Musées Royaux des Beaux-Arts de Belgique

160. J. Provost. Altarpiece of the Legends of St. Anthony of Padua and St. Bonaventure, Reverses of the Shutters. *Brussels, Musées Royaux des Beaux-Arts de Belgique*

Plate
176

161 | Add. 274

161 | Add. 274

161. J. Provost. St. Andrew, with Reverse. *Haarlem, Bisschoppelijk Museum, on loan from the Dienst voor 's Rijks Verspreide Kunstvoorwerpen, The Hague.* Add. 274. J. Provost. St. Christopher, with Reverse. *Madrid, Museo del Prado*

Plate
177

162 | 163
164 | 165

162. J. Provost. St. Jerome. *Present location unknown.* 163. J. Provost. St. Andrew. *Amsterdam, P. de Boer collection.* 164. J. Provost. Virgin Enthroned. *Present location unknown.* 165. J. Provost. Virgin and Child. *Present location unknown*

Plate
178

166	167
167

166. J. Provost. Virgin and Child. *Cremona, Museo Civico.* 167. J. Provost. Virgin and Child, with Reverse. *Piacenza, Galleria Alberoni*

Plate
179

168. J. Provost. Virgin and Child. *London, National Gallery*

Plate
180

169 | 170
171 | 172

169. J. Provost. Virgin and Child. *Edinburgh, National Galleries of Scotland.* 170. J. Provost. Virgin and Child. *Strasbourg, Musée des Beaux-Arts.* 171. J. Provost. Virgin and Child. *Present location unknown.* 172. J. Provost. Virgin and Child. *Present location unknown*

174 / 175 | 176

174. J. Provost. Virgin and Child. *Darmstadt, Hessisches Landesmuseum.* 175. J. Provost. Virgin and Child. *Leningrad, The Hermitage.* 176. J. Provost. Virgin and Child. *Karlsruhe, Staatliche Kunsthalle*

Plate
182

177. J. Provost. Virgin in the Clouds. *Leningrad, The Hermitage*

177. J. Provost. Virgin in the Clouds, Detail. *Leningrad, The Hermitage*

Plate
184

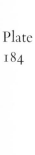

178. J. Provost. Virgin Enthroned. *The Hague, Koninklijk Kabinet van Schilderijen, Mauritshuis, on loan from the Rijksmuseum, Amsterdam*

179 | 180
179 | 180

179. J. Provost. Virgin and St. Joseph, with Reverse. *Banbury, Upton House (National Trust).* 180. J. Provost. Portrait of a Man, with Reverse. *Paris, Musée du Louvre*

Plate
186

182 | 181

183 |

182. J. Provost. Portrait of a Donor. *Philadelphia, Pa., John G. Johnson Collection.* 181. J. Provost. Portrait of a Donatrix. *Castagnola, Thyssen-Bornemisza Collection, Schloss Rohoncz Foundation.* 183. J. Provost. Portrait of a Man. *Kreuzlingen, Switzerland, Heinz Kisters collection*

184. Bruges Master of 1500. Crucifixion, Christ Carrying the Cross, Lamentation. *Bruges, Museum of the Church of the Saviour*

Plate
188

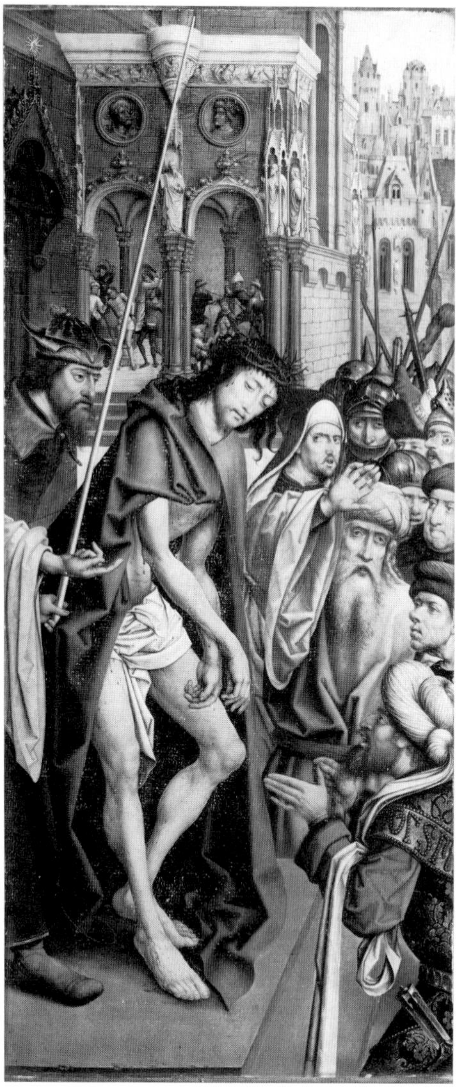

185 | 186

185. Bruges Master of 1500. Christ Shown to the People. *London, National Gallery.* 186. Bruges Master of 1500. The Miracle of St. Anthony. *Madrid, Museo del Prado*

Plate
189

187. Master of the André Madonna. Virgin and Child. *Paris, Musée Jacquemart-André*

Plate
190

188 | 189

188. Master of the André Madonna. Virgin and Child. *Castagnola, Thyssen-Bornemisza Collection, Schloss Rohoncz Foundation.* 189. Master of the André Madonna. Virgin and Child. *Present location unknown.*

190. Master of St. Sang. Altarpiece of the Adoration of the Magi. *Present location unknown*

Plate
192

191. Master of St. Sang. Altarpiece of the Adoration of the Magi. *Hugenpoet Castle, Rhine Province, Baron Fürstenberg collection*

192. Master of St. Sang. Altarpiece of the Christ Shown to the People. *Madrid, Museo del Prado*

Plate
194

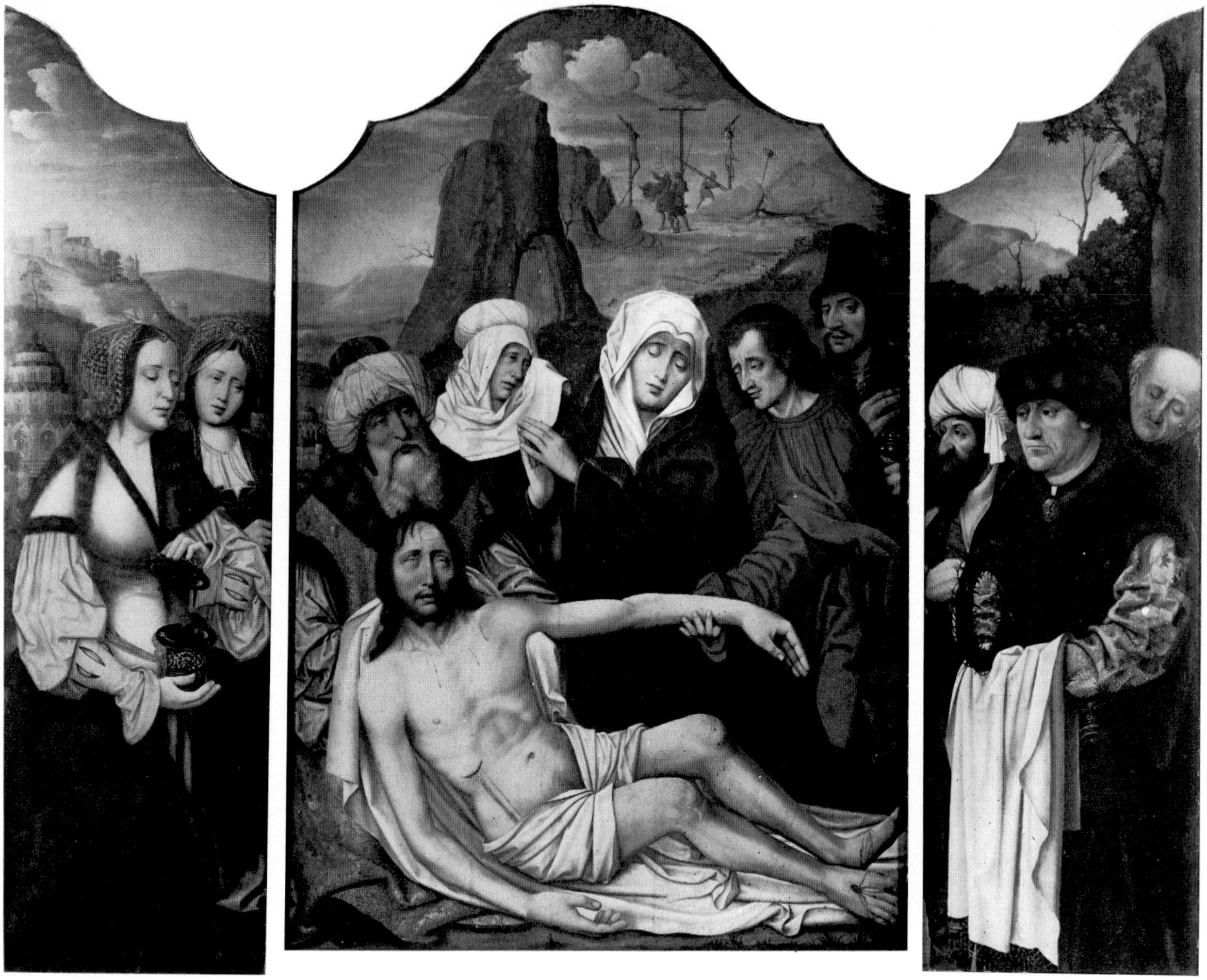

193. Master of St. Sang. Altarpiece of the Lamentation. *Bruges, Chapel of St. Sang*

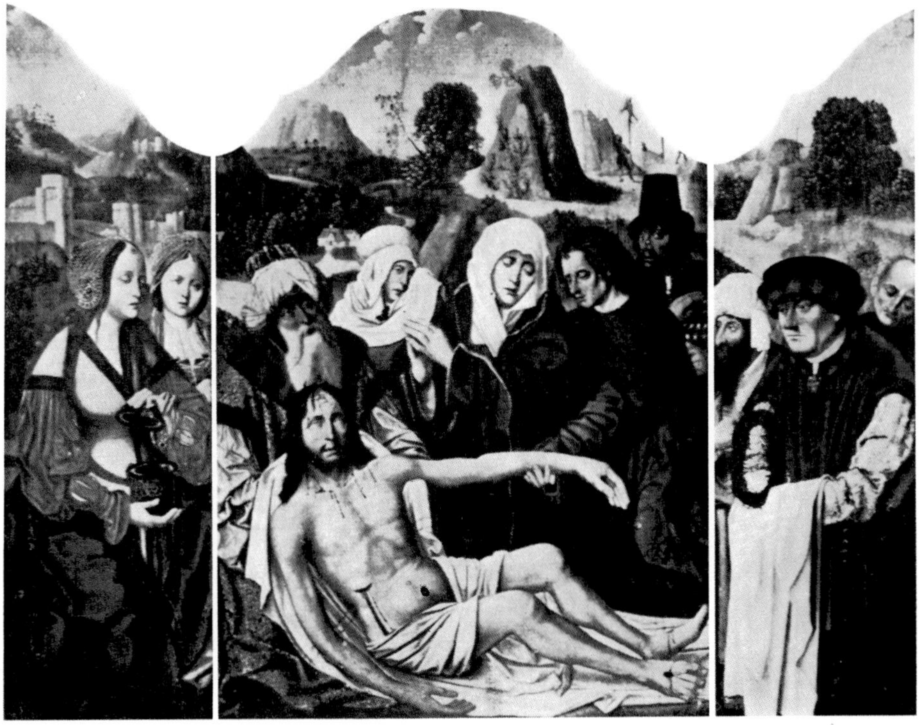

193 a
———
193 b

193 a. Master of St. Sang. Altarpiece of the Lamentation. *Present location unknown.*
193 b. Master of St. Sang. Altarpiece of the Lamentation. *Present location unknown*

194
196

194. Master of St. Sang. Altarpiece of the Holy Family. *Hamburg, Kunsthalle.* 196. Master of St. Sang. A Pair of Shutters, St. Barbara, St. Catherine. *Cleveland, Ohio, Cleveland Museum of Art, John L. Severance Bequest*

195. Master of St. Sang. Altarpiece of the Virgin. *Bruges, Church of St. James*

Plate 198

195. Master of St. Sang. Altarpiece of the Virgin, Centrepiece. *Bruges, Church of St. James*

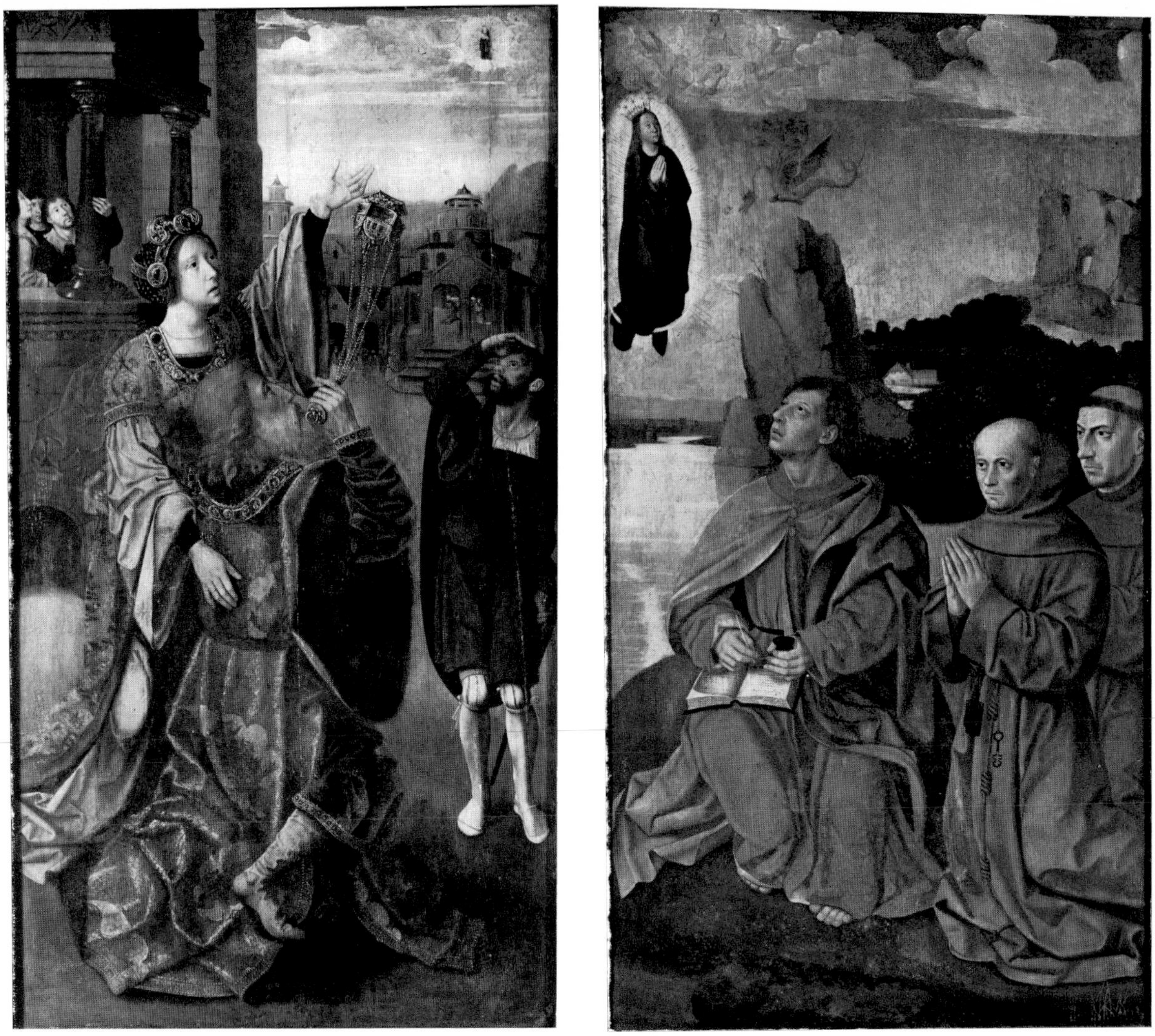

195. Master of St. Sang. Altarpiece of the Virgin, Shutters, The Emperor Augustus with the Sibyl, St. John on the Island of Patmos. *Bruges, Church of St. James*

Plate
200

197
———
199

197. Master of St. Sang. Adoration of the Magi. *Milan, Pinacoteca Ambrosiana.* 199. Master of St. Sang. Christ Shown to the People. *Lisbon, Mrs. Ricardo Espírito Santo Silva collection*

200. Master of St. Sang. Christ Carrying the Cross. *Greenville, S. C., Bob Jones University, Collection of Religious Paintings*

Plate
202

201 | 203
202 |

201. Master of St. Sang. The Almighty with the Dead Saviour. *Brussels, Musées Royaux des Beaux-Arts de Belgique.* 202. Master of St. Sang. Christ with the Virgin and St. John. *Present location unknown.* 203. Master of St. Sang. Virgin and Child. *Houston, Texas, Museum of Fine Arts, Edith A. and Percy S. Straus Collection*

204 | 205
206 | 207

204. Master of St. Sang. Virgin and Child. *Present location unknown.* 205. Master of St. Sang. Virgin and Child. *Present location unknown.* 206. Master of St. Sang. Virgin and Child. *Present location unknown.* 207. Master of St. Sang. The Holy Family. *Present location unknown*

Plate 204

208 | 209
210

208. Master of St. Sang. Virgin Enthroned. *Antwerp, Koninklijk Museum voor Schone Kunsten.* 209. Master of St. Sang. Virgin and Child. *Palermo, Galleria Nazionale.* 210. Master of St. Sang. The Holy Family. *Hamburg, Kunsthalle*

211 | 212
213

211. Master of St. Sang. Virgin and Child with St. Bernard. *Brussels, Musées Royaux des Beaux-Arts de Belgique.*
212. Master of St. Sang. St. Luke Painting the Virgin. *Cambridge, Mass., Busch-Reisinger Museum, Harvard University.*
213. Master of St. Sang. Virgin and Child with St. Anne. *Frankfurt-on-Main, Staedelsches Kunstinstitut*

Plate
206

215 | 214
214 a

215. Master of St. Sang. Lucretia. *Vienna, Gemäldegalerie der Akademie der Bildenden Künste.* 214. Master of St. Sang. Lucretia. *Present location unknown.* 214 a. Master of St. Sang. Lucretia. *Present location unknown*

216 | 217 a
217 b

216. Master of St. Sang. Lucretia. *Budapest, Museum of Fine Arts.* 217 a. Master of St. Sang. Lucretia. *Present location unknown.* 217 b. Master of St. Sang. Lucretia. *Munich, Bayerische Staatsgemäldesammlungen, Alte Pinakothek*

Plate
208

218
———
218 a

218. J. Patenier. Altarpiece of the Virgin and Child. *Frankfurt-on-Main, W. Kaus collection.* 218 a. J. Patenier, Copy. Altarpiece of the Virgin and Child, Centrepiece. Present location unknown

218. J. Patenier. Altarpiece of the Virgin and Child, Centrepiece. *Frankfurt-on-Main, W. Kaus collection*

Plate
210

218 J. Patenier. Atarpiece of the Virgin and Child, Shutters, St. John the Baptist, The Pope Cornelius. *Frankfurt-on-Main, W. Kaus collection*

219

Supp. 267 | Supp. 268

219. J. Patenier. Landscape with Sodom on Fire. *Rotterdam, Museum Boymans-van Beuningen, on loan from the Dienst voor 's Rijks Verspreide Kunstvoorwerpen, The Hague.* Supp. 267. J. Patenier. Landscape with Sodom on Fire. *Oxford, Ashmolean Museum, Department of Western Art.* Supp. 268. J. Patenier. Landscape with Sodom on Fire. *Zurich, Dr. H. C. Walter Boveri collection*

220. J. Patenier. St. John the Baptist Preaching. *Philadelphia, Pa., Museum of Art*

220 a
220 b

220 a. J. Patenier. St. John the Baptist Preaching. *Brussels, Musées Royaux des Beaux-Arts de Belgique.* 220 b. J. Patenier. St. John the Baptist Preaching. *Present location unknown*

222. J. Patenier. Landscape with St. John the Baptist Preaching. *Uppsala, University*

223. J. Patenier. Landscape with the Baptism of Christ. *Uppsala, University*

Plate
216

221. J. Patenier. The Baptism of Christ. *Vienna, Kunsthistorisches Museum*

224
225

224. J. Patenier. The Crucifixion. *Portland, Oregon, Portland Art Museum.* 225. J. Patenier. Christ Carrying the Cross. *Present location unknown*

Plate
218

226. J. Patenier. Assumption of the Virgin. *Philadelphia, Pa., John G. Johnson Collection*

227 | 227 a / 228

227. J. Patenier. Virgin and Child. *Present location unknown* . 227 a. J. Patenier, Copy. Virgin and Child. *Present location unknown*. 228. J. Patenier. Flight into Egypt. *Minneapolis, Institute of Arts, The William Hood Dunwoody Fund*

Plate
220

231. J. Patenier. Flight into Egypt. *Antwerp, Koninklijk Museum voor Schone Kunsten*

232. J. Patenier. Virgin and Child, Resting on the Flight. *Castagnola, Thyssen-Bornemisza Collection, Schloss Rohoncz Foundation*

Plate
222

233. J. Patenier. Virgin and Child, Resting on the Flight. *Antwerp, Museum Ridder Smidt van Gelder*

234. J. Patenier. Virgin and Child, Resting on the Flight. *Philadelphia, Pa., John G. Johnson Collection*

235. J. Patenier. Virgin and Child, Resting on the Flight. *Madrid, Museo del Prado*

235. J. Patenier. Virgin and Child, Resting on the Flight, Detail. *Madrid, Museo del Prado*

Plate
226

237. J. Patenier. Virgin and Child, Resting on the Flight. *Berlin-Dahlem, Gemäldegalerie der Staatlichen Museen*

237. J. Patenier. Virgin and Child, Resting on the Flight, Detail. *Berlin-Dahlem, Gemäldegalerie der Staatlichen Museen*

Plate
228

238
———
239

238. J. Patenier. Virgin and Child, Resting on the Flight. *Stockholm, Nationalmuseum.* 239. J. Patenier. St. Jerome. *Karlsruhe, Staatliche Kunsthalle*

241
241 a

241. J. Patenier. St. Jerome. *Present location unknown.* 241 a. J. Patenier. St. Jerome. *Chambésy-Geneva, Mr. and Mrs. T. Kreuger collection*

Plate
230

240. J. Patenier. St. Jerome. *Madrid, Museo del Prado*

240. J. Patenier. St. Jerome, Detail. *Madrid, Museo del Prado*

Plate
232

243
243 b | 251

243. J. Patenier. St. Jerome. *Wuppertal-Elberfeld, Von der Heydt-Museum.* 243b. J. Patenier. St. Jerome. *Zurich, Kunsthaus, Ruzicka-Stiftung.* 251. J. Patenier. Assumption of the Egyptian Mary. *Zurich, Kunsthaus, Ruzicka-Stiftung*

243 a. J. Patenier. St. Jerome. *London, National Gallery*

Plate
234

242
244

242. J. Patenier. St. Jerome. *Present location unknown.* 244. J. Patenier. St. Jerome. *Kansas City, Mo., Nelson Gallery-Atkins Museum, Nelson Fund*

246. J. Patenier. St. Christopher. *El Escorial, Real Palacio y Monasterio de S. Lorenzo*

Plate
236

246. J. Patenier. St. Christopher, Detail. *El Escorial, Real Palacio y Monasterio de S. Lorenzo*

246. J. Patenier. St. Christopher, Detail. *El Escorial, Real Palacio y Monasterio de S. Lorenzo*

Plate
238

245
245 a

245. J. Patenier. St. Jerome. *Paris, Musée du Louvre.* 245 a. J. Patenier. St. Jerome. *Venice, Cà d'Oro (Giorgio Franchetti Galleria)*

247 | 248
249

247. J. Patenier. St. Christopher. *Present location unknown.* 248. J. Patenier. St. Christopher. *Palermo, Baron Gabrielle Chiaramonte Bordonaro collection.* 249. J. Patenier. Two Hermits in a Landscape. *Present location unknown*

Plate
240

250
250 a

250. J. Patenier. Martyrdom of St. Catherine. *Vienna, Kunsthistorisches Museum.* 250 a. J. Patenier. Martyrdom of St. Catherine. *Belgium, S. Simon collection*

Plate
241

252
254

252. J. Patenier. Assumption of the Egyptian Mary. *Present location unknown.* 254. J. Patenier. Tobias and the Angel. *Basle, Öffentliche Kunstsammlung*

Plate
242

253. J. Patenier. River Styx. *Madrid, Museo del Prado*

255
256

255. J. Patenier. Stormy Seascape with Rocky Shores. *Belgium, S. Simon collection.*
256. J. Patenier. Landscape with Hunting Scenes. *Geneva, Mr. and Mrs. C.H. Wilmers collection*

Plate
244

257. J. Patenier. Landscape with Genrelike Figures. *Present location unknown*

Supp. A. J. Joest. Shutters of the Brömse Altarpiece. *Lübeck, Church of St. James* (see p. 48)

Plate
246

Supp. 258. J. Joest. Altarpiece of the Nativity. *Munich, Bayerische Staatsgemäldesammlungen, Alte Pinakothek*

Supp. 260. J. Van Cleve. Portrait of a Gentleman. *Düsseldorf, Kunstmuseum, Bentinck-Thyssen collection*

Plate
248

Supp. 259 | Supp. 261

Supp. 259. J. van Cleve. Portrait of a Gentleman. *Present location unknown.* Supp. 261. J. van Cleve. Portrait of a Lady. *Present location unknown*

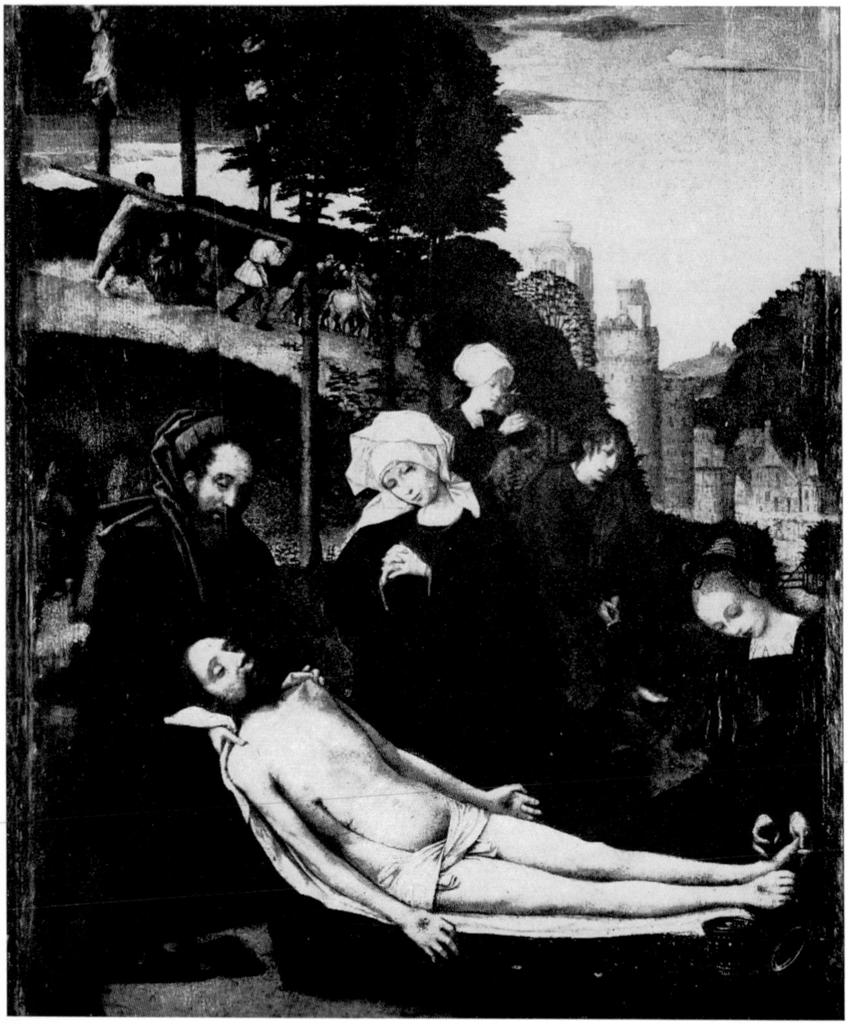

Supp. 264 | Supp. 265

Supp. 264. J. Provost. Lamentation. *Palermo, Galleria Nazionale.* Supp. 265. J. Provost. Angel of the Annunciation. *Present location unknown*

Supp. 266. J. Patenier. Altarpiece of St. Jerome. *New York, Metropolitan Museum of Art, The Fletcher Fund*

Supp. 266. J. Patenier. Altarpiece of St. Jerome, Centrepiece. *New York, Metropolitan Museum of Art, The Fletcher Fund*

Plate
252

Supp. 269
Add. 271

Supp. 269. J. Patenier. Landscape. *Present location unknown.* Add. 271. J. Joest. The Nativity. Drawing. *Leningrad, The Hermitage*

Add. 272. J. Van Cleve. Flight into Egypt. *Ponce, Puerto Rico, Museo de Arte*

A. Portrait of Joachim Patenier. Engraving from *D. Lampsonius «Pictorum Aliquot... Effigies». Antwerp*, 1572 (see p. 100)